William Shakespeare, William James Rolfe

Comedy of Much Ado about Nothing

Edited with Notes by William J. Rolfe

William Shakespeare, William James Rolfe

Comedy of Much Ado about Nothing
Edited with Notes by William J. Rolfe

ISBN/EAN: 9783744776059

Printed in Europe, USA, Canada, Australia, Japan

Cover: Foto ©Thomas Meinert / pixelio.de

More available books at **www.hansebooks.com**

SHAKESPEARE'S

COMEDY OF

MUCH ADO ABOUT NOTHING.

Edited, with Notes,

by

WILLIAM J. ROLFE, Litt. D.,
FORMERLY HEAD MASTER OF THE HIGH SCHOOL, CAMBRIDGE, MASS.

WITH ENGRAVINGS.

NEW YORK:
HARPER & BROTHERS, PUBLISHERS,
FRANKLIN SQUARE.
1895.

ENGLISH CLASSICS.

Edited by WM. J. ROLFE, Litt. D.

Illustrated. 16mo, Cloth, 56 cents per volume; Paper, 40 cents per volume.

SHAKESPEARE'S WORKS.

- The Merchant of Venice.
- Othello.
- Julius Cæsar.
- A Midsummer-Night's Dream.
- Macbeth.
- Hamlet.
- Much Ado about Nothing.
- Romeo and Juliet.
- As You Like It.
- The Tempest.
- Twelfth Night.
- The Winter's Tale.
- King John.
- Richard II.
- Henry IV. Part I.
- Henry IV. Part II.
- Henry V.
- Henry VI. Part I.
- Henry VI. Part II.
- Henry VI. Part III.
- Richard III.
- Henry VIII.
- King Lear.
- The Taming of the Shrew.
- All 's Well that Ends Well.
- Coriolanus.
- The Comedy of Errors.
- Cymbeline.
- Antony and Cleopatra.
- Measure for Measure.
- Merry Wives of Windsor.
- Love's Labour 's Lost.
- Two Gentlemen of Verona.
- Timon of Athens.
- Troilus and Cressida.
- Pericles, Prince of Tyre.
- The Two Noble Kinsmen.
- Venus and Adonis, Lucrece, etc.
- Sonnets.
- Titus Andronicus.

GOLDSMITH'S SELECT POEMS. BROWNING'S SELECT POEMS.
GRAY'S SELECT POEMS. BROWNING'S SELECT DRAMAS.
MINOR POEMS OF JOHN MILTON. MACAULAY'S LAYS OF ANCIENT ROME
WORDSWORTH'S SELECT POEMS.

PUBLISHED BY HARPER & BROTHERS, NEW YORK.

☞ *The above works are for sale by all booksellers, or they will be sent by* HARPER & BROTHERS *to any address on receipt of price as quoted. If ordered sent by mail, 10 per cent. should be added to the price to cover cost of postage.*

CONTENTS.

	PAGE
INTRODUCTION TO MUCH ADO ABOUT NOTHING	9
I. THE HISTORY OF THE PLAY	9
II. THE SOURCES OF THE PLOT	10
III. CRITICAL COMMENTS ON THE PLAY	13
MUCH ADO ABOUT NOTHING	27
ACT I	29
" II	42
" III	63
" IV	81
" V	95
NOTES	115

EXTERIOR OF THE CATHEDRAL OF MESSINA.

MESSINA, FROM THE SEA.

INTRODUCTION
TO
MUCH ADO ABOUT NOTHING.

I. THE HISTORY OF THE PLAY.

THE first edition of *Much Ado About Nothing* was a quarto, published in 1600 with the following title-page:

Much adoe about | Nothing. | *As it hath been sundrie times publikely* | acted by the right honourable, the Lord | Chamberlaine his seruants. | *Written by William Shakespeare.* | London | Printed by V. S. for Andrew Wise, and | William Aspley. | 1600.

The earliest known reference to the play is in the Registers of the Stationers' Company, among some miscellaneous memoranda at the beginning of Volume C.* The memorandum follows one dated May 27th, 1600, and is thus given by Arber:

* See our ed. of *As You Like It*, p. 10.

4. Augustí

A... 'il... rl... a booke
ÍII NK Y ťie FHFFY / a booke
Eu ry man in his humour / a booke
The commedie of 'muche a Doo about nothing' a booke /

} to be staied.

The year is not given, but there can be little doubt that it was 1600.

In the same volume, among the regular entries of the year 1600, we find the following:

23 Augustí

Andrew Wyse
William Aspley

Entred for their copies vnder the handes of the wardens Two bookes. the one called *Muche a Doo about nothinge*. Th[e] other the *second parte of the history of kinge HENRY the IIIJ*th *with the humours of Sir JOHN FFALLSTAFF*: Wrytten by master *SHAKESPERE* - - - - - xij^d

This, by the way, is the first occurrence of the poet's name in these Registers.

The quarto of 1600 was, on the whole, well printed; and no other edition of the play is known to have been issued previous to the publication of the Folio of 1623. The printers of the latter appear to have used a copy of the quarto belonging to the library of the theatre and corrected for the purposes of the stage; but the changes are for the most part very slight and seldom for the better, as will be seen by our *Notes* below.

As the play is not mentioned in Meres's list of 1598 (see our ed. of *A. Y. L.* p. 10), while it had been "sundrie times" acted before its publication in August, 1600, it was probably written in 1599.

II. THE SOURCES OF THE PLOT.

The earlier incidents of the serious portion of the plot may have been taken from the story of Ariodante and Ginevra in Ariosto's *Orlando Furioso*, canto v.; where Polinesso, in order to revenge himself on the princess Ginevra (who has rejected his suit and pledged her troth to Ariodante) induces her attendant Dalinda to personate the princess and to appear at night at a balcony to which he ascends by a rope-ladder in sight of Ariodante, whom he has stationed there to witness the infidelity of Ginevra. A translation of this story by Peter Beverley was entered on the Stationers' Registers in 1565-6, and was doubtless printed soon afterwards; and in 1582-3 "A History of Ariodante and Geneuora" was "shewed before her Matie on Shrovetuesdaie at night, enacted by Mr. Mulcasters children." According to Sir John Harrington, the same story had been "written in English verse" by George Turbervile, before the publication of his own translation of the *Orlando* in 1591. Spenser had also introduced the tale, with some variations. in the *Faerie Queene* (ii. 4. 17 fol.), and this part of the poem was published in 1590.

It is more probable, however, that the source from which Shakespeare drew this part of his materials was the 22d Novel of Bandello, which had been translated into French by Belleforest in his *Histoires Tragiques* (see our ed. of *Hamlet*, p. 13), and probably also rendered into English, though the version has not come down to our day. In Bandello's story, as in the play, the scene is laid at Messina; the father of the slandered maiden is Lionato; and the friend of her lover is Don Piero, or Pedro. How closely the poet has followed the novel will be seen from the outline of the latter given by Staunton: "Don Piero of Arragon returns from a victorious campaign, and, with the gallant cavalier Timbreo di Cardona, is at Messina. Timbreo falls in love with Fenicia, the daughter of Lionato di Lionati, a gentleman of Messina, and, like Claudio in the play, courts her by proxy. He is successful in his suit, and the lovers are betrothed; but the course of true love is impeded by one Girondo, a disappointed admirer of the lady, who determines to prevent the marriage. In pursuance of this object, he insinuates to Timbreo that Fenicia is false, and offers to show him a stranger scaling her chamber window. The unhappy lover consents to watch; and at the appointed hour Girondo and a servant in the plot pass him disguised, and the latter is seen to ascend a ladder and enter the house of Lionato. In an agony of rage and jealousy, Timbreo in the morning accuses the lady of disloyalty, and rejects the alliance. Fenicia falls into a swoon; a dangerous illness supervenes; and the father, to stifle all rumours hurtful to her fame, removes her to a retired house of his brother, proclaims her death, and solemnly performs her funeral obsequies. Girondo is now struck with remorse at having 'slandered to death' a creature so innocent and beautiful. He confesses his treachery to Timbreo, and both determine to restore the reputation of the lost one, and undergo any penance her family may impose. Lionato is merciful, and requires only from Timbreo that he shall wed a lady whom he recommends, and whose face shall be concealed till the marriage ceremony is over. The *dénouement* is obvious. Timbreo espouses the mysterious fair one, and finds in her his injured, loving, and beloved Fenicia."

The comic portion of the play is Shakespeare's own, as indeed is everything else in it except this mere skeleton of tragic incident. Claudio and Hero, Don Pedro and Don John, are as really his own creations as Benedick and Beatrice, Dogberry and Verges, who have no part in Bandello's novel or Ariosto's poem. As Knight remarks, "Ariosto made this story a tale of chivalry, Spenser a lesson of high and solemn morality, Bandello an interesting love-romance; it was for Shakspere to surround the main incident with those accessories which he could nowhere borrow, and to make of it such a comedy as no other man has made—a comedy, not of manners or of sentiment, but of *life* viewed under its profoundest aspects, whether of the grave or the ludicrous."

III. CRITICAL COMMENTS ON THE PLAY.
[*From Schlegel's "Dramatic Literature."**]

The manner in which the innocent Hero before the altar at the moment of the wedding, and in the presence of her family and many witnesses, is put to shame by a most degrading charge, false indeed, yet clothed with every appearance of truth, is a grand piece of theatrical effect in the true and justifiable sense. The impression would have been too tragical had not Shakspeare carefully softened it, in order to prepare for a fortunate catastrophe. The discovery of the plot against Hero has been already partly made, though not by the persons interested; and the poet has contrived, by means of the blundering simplicity of a couple of constables and watchmen, to convert the arrest and the examination of the guilty individuals into scenes full of the most delightful amusement. There is also a second piece of theatrical effect not inferior to the first, where Claudio, now convinced of his error, and in obedience to the penance laid on his fault, thinking to give his hand to a relation of his injured bride, whom he supposes dead, discovers, on her unmasking, Hero herself. The extraordinary success of this play in Shakspeare's own day, and even since in England, is, however, to be ascribed more particularly to the parts of Benedick and Beatrice, two humorous beings, who incessantly attack each other with all the resources of raillery. Avowedly rebels to love, they are both entangled in its net by a merry plot of their friends to make them believe that each is the object of the secret passion of the other. Some one or other, not overstocked with penetration, has objected to the same artifice being twice used in entrapping them; the drollery, however, lies in the very symmetry of the deception. Their friends attribute the whole effect to their own device,

---

* *Lectures on Dramatic Art and Literature*, by A. W. Schlegel; Black's translation, revised by Morrison (London, 1846), p. 386.

but the exclusive direction of their raillery against each other is in itself a proof of a growing inclination. Their witty vivacity does not even abandon them in the avowal of love; and their behaviour only assumes a serious appearance for the purpose of defending the slandered Hero. This is exceedingly well imagined; the lovers of jesting must fix a point beyond which they are not to indulge in their humour, if they would not be mistaken for buffoons by trade.

[*From Gervinus's "Shakespeare Commentaries."**]

Bandello's tale did not afford the poet even a hint of any moral view of the story; it is a bald narrative, containing nothing which could assist in the understanding of the Shakespearian piece. In *As You Like It* he had to conceal the vast moralizing of the source from which he drew his material; here, on the other hand, he had to strike the latent spark within the material. The story of Claudio and Hero was transferred by Shakespeare from the shallow novel into life; he dived into the nature of the incidents; he investigated the probable character of the beings among whom it was imaginable; he found the key-note by means of which he could bring the whole into harmony. The subject expanded in his hands; the main action received an explanatory prelude; the principal characters (Hero and Claudio) obtained an important counterpart in the connection between Benedick and Beatrice, which is entirely Shakespeare's property; these characters gained an importance even beyond the principal ones; the plot, as is ever the case with our poet, and as Coleridge† has especially pointed out in this

---

* *Shakespeare Commentaries*, by Dr. G. G. Gervinus, translated by F. E. Bunnètt; revised ed. (London, 1875), p. 406 fol. (by permission). A few slight verbal changes have been made by the editor.

† Coleridge remarks: "The interest in the plot is always on account of the characters, not *vice versâ*, as in almost all other writers; the plot is a mere canvas and no more. Hence arises the true justification of the

play, gave place to the characterization; the question seems almost what manner of men made the *much ado* about nothing, rather than the *nothing* about which *ado* was made. The whole stress seems to lie, not in the plot, not in the outward interest of the catastrophe, but in the moral significance which the disturbance caused by Don John exercises upon the two engagements which are concluded and prepared, and again dissolved and left unconfirmed, or rather upon the beings who have entered into these engagements. . . .

The poet has with extraordinary skill so arranged and introduced the tragic incident that the painful impression which is perhaps too sensible in the reading is lost in the acting. He omitted upon the stage the scene of Claudio's agitation on overhearing Hero, in order that he might thus avoid the gloom, and not weaken the comic scene in which a trap is laid for the listening Beatrice. The burlesque scenes of the constables are introduced with the impending tragic events, that they may afford a counterbalance to them and prevent them from having too lively an effect on the spectator. But, above all, we are already aware that the authors of the deception are in custody before Hero's disgrace in the church takes place; we know, therefore, that all the ado about her crime and death is for nothing. This tact of the poet in the construction of his comedy corresponds with that in the design of Claudio's character, and in the unusually happy contrast which he has presented to him in Benedick. Shakespeare has so blended the elements in

same stratagem being used in regard to Benedick and Beatrice—the vanity in each being alike. Take away from *Much Ado About Nothing* all that which is not indispensable to the plot, . . . take away Benedick, Beatrice, Dogberry, and the reaction of the former on the character of Hero, and what will remain? In other writers the main agent of the plot is always the prominent character; in Shakspeare it is so, or is not so, as the character is in itself calculated, or not calculated, to form the plot. Don John is the mainspring of the plot of this play; but he is merely shown and then withdrawn."

Claudio's nature, he has given such a good foundation of honour and self-reliance to his unstable mind and fickle youth, that we cannot, with all our disapprobation of his conduct, be doubtful as to his character. Changeable as he is, he continues stable in no choice of friends and loved ones, since he had never continuously tested them; at the slightest convulsion of events he is overpowered by first impressions, and he is without the strength of will to search to the bottom of things. This would be an odious and despicable character, if the changeableness were not tempered by the sensitiveness of a tender feeling of honour. Our interest in Claudio is secured by this blending of the moral elements in his nature; but the foundation for a comic character does not appear to lie either in him or in the whole action in which he is implicated. If we separate it from the rest, we shall retain a painful and not a cheerful impression. The poet has thus added the connection between Benedick and Beatrice, in order to produce a merry counterbalance to the more serious and primary element of the play, and to make the former predominate. The same self-love and the same spoiling by prosperity fall to the lot of these two characters as to that of Claudio; but, instead of his changeableness, we see in them only what, with a fine distinction, we should (with Benedick) call giddiness. We connect the idea of changeableness with a continual wavering after resolutions taken; that of giddiness with unstable opinions and inclinations before the same: changeableness manifests itself in actions, it is productive of pernicious consequences, and for this reason causes contempt and hatred; giddiness manifests itself only in contrary processes of the mind, which are by nature harmless, and this is the reason why it offers excellent material for comedy. Few characters, therefore, on the stage have such truly comic character as Benedick and Beatrice, and they have not lost their popularity in England even to the present day. Shakespeare's contemporary, Leonard

Digges, speaks of them together with Falstaff and Malvolio as the favourites of the public of that day; as characters which filled pit, gallery, and boxes in a moment, while Ben Jonson's comedies frequently did not pay for fire and doorkeeper....

It would have been difficult for Benedick and Beatrice in the midst of their hostile raillery to come to a serious explanation; the concluding scene itself proves this, after events have led to this explanation. This is brought about by the heartless scene which Claudio prepares for Hero in the church. The better nature of Beatrice bursts forth to light amid this base ill-treatment. Her true love for Hero, her deep conviction of her innocence, her anger at the deliberate malice of her public dishonour, stir up her whole soul and make it a perfect contrast to what we have seen in her hitherto.... Sorrow for Hero and for the honour of her house makes Beatrice gentle, tender, and weakened into tears; this "happy hour" facilitates to both their serious confession. But at the same time this hour of misfortune tests these beings, accustomed as they are only to jest and raillery, by a heavy trial, in the sustaining of which we are convinced that these gifted natures are not devoid of that seriousness which regards no earnest situation with frivolity. We should more readily have imputed this gift to Claudio, but we find it existing far more in the humorous couple who had not taken life so lightly, and who had at last accustomed themselves to truth. Beatrice places before Benedick the cruel choice between her esteem and love and his connection with his friend. His great confidence in her, and in *her* unshaken confidence in Hero, led him to make his difficult decision, in which he acts with vigour and prudence, very differently from Claudio in his difficulties. Beatrice, the untamed colt, learns at the same time how the most masculine woman cannot dispense with assistance in certain cases; she has moreover seen her Benedick in a position in which he responds to her ideal of a man, in whom mirth and seriousness should be justly blended. . . . Benedick goes off the stage with a confession of his giddiness, but it is a giddiness overcome, and we have no reason to be anxious either for the constancy or for the peaceableness of this pair. The poet has bestowed upon them two names of happy augury. . . .

[*From Mrs. Jameson's "Characteristics of Women."**]

Shakspeare has exhibited in Beatrice a spirited and faithful portrait of the fine lady of his own time. The deportment, language, manners, and allusions are those of a particular class in a particular age; but the individual and dramatic character which forms the groundwork is strongly discriminated, and being taken from general nature, belongs to every age. In Beatrice, high intellect and high animal spirits meet, and excite each other like fire and air. In her wit (which is brilliant without being imaginative) there is a touch of insolence, not unfrequent in women when the wit predominates over reflection and imagination. In her temper, too, there is a slight infusion of the termagant; and her satirical humour plays with such an unrespective levity over all subjects alike that it required a profound knowledge of women to bring such a character within the pale of our sympathy. But Beatrice, though wilful, is not wayward; she is volatile, not unfeeling. She has not only an exuberance of wit and gayety, but of heart and soul and energy of spirit; and is no more like the fine ladies of modern comedy — whose wit consists in a temporary allusion, or a play upon words, and whose petulance is displayed in a toss of the head, a flirt of the fan, or a flourish of the pocket-handkerchief — than one of our modern dandies is like Sir Philip Sidney.

In Beatrice, Shakspeare has contrived that the poetry of the character shall not only soften, but heighten its comic effect. We are not only inclined to forgive Beatrice all her

* American ed. (Boston, 1857), p. 99 fol.

scornful airs, all her biting jests, all her assumption of superiority; but they amuse and delight us the more when we find her, with all the headlong simplicity of a child, falling at once into the snare laid for her affections; when we see *her* who thought a man of God's making not good enough for her, who disdained to be o'ermastered by "a piece of valiant dust," stooping like the rest of her sex, vailing her proud spirit and taming her wild heart to the loving hand of him whom she had scorned, flouted, and misused "past the endurance of a block." And we are yet more completely won by her generous enthusiastic attachment to her cousin. When the father of Hero believes the tale of her guilt; when Claudio, her lover, without remorse or a lingering doubt, consigns her to shame; when the Friar remains silent, and the generous Benedick himself knows not what to say, Beatrice, confident in her affections, and guided only by the impulses of her own feminine heart, sees through the inconsistency, the impossibility of the charge, and exclaims, without a moment's hesitation,

"O, on my soul, my cousin is belied!"

Schlegel, in his remarks on the play, has given us an amusing instance of that sense of reality with which we are impressed by Shakspeare's characters. He says of Benedick and Beatrice, as if he had known them personally, that the exclusive direction of their pointed raillery against each other "is a proof of a growing inclination." This is not unlikely; and the same inference would lead us to suppose that this mutual inclination had commenced before the opening of the play. The very first words uttered by Beatrice are an inquiry after Benedick, though expressed with her usual arch impertinence:—

"I pray you, is Signior Montanto returned from the wars, or no?"

"I pray you, how many hath he killed and eaten in these wars? But how many hath he killed? for indeed I promised to eat all of his killing."

And in the unprovoked hostility with which she falls upon him in his absence, in the pertinacity and bitterness of her satire, there is certainly great argument that he occupies much more of her thoughts than she would have been willing to confess, even to herself. In the same manner Benedick betrays a lurking partiality for his fascinating enemy: he shows that he has looked upon her with no careless eye when he says,

"There's her cousin [meaning Beatrice], an she were not possessed with a fury, excels her as much in beauty as the first of May does the last of December."

Infinite skill, as well as humour, is shown in making this pair of airy beings the exact counterpart of each other; but of the two portraits, that of Benedick is by far the most pleasing, because the independence and gay indifference of temper, the laughing defiance of love and marriage, the satirical freedom of expression, common to both, are more becoming to the masculine than to the feminine character. Any woman might love such a cavalier as Benedick, and be proud of his affection; his valour, his wit, and his gayety sit so gracefully upon him! and his light scoffs against the power of love are but just sufficient to render more piquant the conquest of this "heretic in despite of beauty." But a man might well be pardoned who should shrink from encountering such a spirit as that of Beatrice, unless, indeed, he had "served an apprenticeship to the taming-school." The wit of Beatrice is less good humoured than that of Benedick; or, from the difference of sex, appears so. It is observable that the power is throughout on her side, and the sympathy and interest on his: which, by reversing the usual order of things, seems to excite us *against the grain*, if I may use such an expression. In all their encounters she constantly gets the better of him, and the gentleman's wits go off halting, if he is not himself fairly *hors de combat*. Beatrice, woman-like, generally has the first word, and will have the last. . . .

In the midst of all this tilting and sparring of their nimble and fiery wits, we find them infinitely anxious for the good opinion of each other, and secretly impatient of each other's scorn; but Beatrice is the most truly indifferent of the two—the most assured of herself. The comic effect produced by their mutual attachment, which, however natural and expected, comes upon us with all the force of a surprise, cannot be surpassed: and how exquisitely characteristic the mutual avowal! . . .

The character of Hero is well contrasted with that of Beatrice, and their mutual attachment is very beautiful and natural. When they are both on the scene together, Hero has but little to say for herself: Beatrice asserts the rule of a master spirit, eclipses her by her mental superiority, abashes her by her raillery, dictates to her, answers for her, and would fain inspire her gentle-hearted cousin with some of her own assurance.

"Yes, faith; it is my cousin's duty to make curtsy and say 'Father, as it please you.'—But yet for all that, cousin, let him be a handsome fellow, or else make another curtsy and say 'Father, as it please me.'"

But Shakspeare knew well how to make one character subordinate to another, without sacrificing the slightest portion of its effect; and Hero, added to her grace and softness, and all the interest which attaches to her as the sentimental heroine of the play, possesses an intellectual beauty of her own. When she has Beatrice at an advantage, she repays her with interest, in the severe but most animated and elegant picture she draws of her cousin's imperious character and unbridled levity of tongue. The portrait is a little overcharged, because administered as a corrective, and intended to be overheard:

"But nature never fram'd a woman's heart
Of prouder stuff than that of Beatrice:
Disdain and scorn ride sparkling in her eyes," etc.

Beatrice never appears to greater advantage than in her

soliloquy after leaving her concealment " in the pleached bower where honeysuckles, ripened by the sun, forbid the sun to enter ;" she exclaims, after listening to this tirade against herself,—

"What fire is in mine ears? Can this be true?
Stand I condemn'd for pride and scorn so much?"

The sense of wounded vanity is lost in better feelings, and she is infinitely more struck by what is said in praise of Benedick, and the history of his supposed love for her, than by the dispraise of herself. The immediate success of the trick is a most natural consequence of the self-assurance and magnanimity of her character; she is so accustomed to assert dominion over the spirits of others that she cannot suspect the possibility of a plot laid against herself. . . .

It is remarkable that, notwithstanding the point and vivacity of the dialogue, few of the speeches of Beatrice are capable of a general application, or engrave themselves distinctly on the memory; they contain more mirth than matter; and though wit be the predominant feature in the dramatic portrait, Beatrice more charms and dazzles us by what she is than by what she *says*. It is not merely her sparkling repartees and saucy jests, it is the soul of wit, and the spirit of gayety informing the whole character—looking out from her brilliant eyes, and laughing on the full lips that pout with scorn—which we have before us, moving and full of life. On the whole, we dismiss Benedick and Beatrice to their matrimonial bonds rather with a sense of amusement than a feeling of congratulation or sympathy; rather with an acknowledgment that they are well-matched and worthy of each other, than with any well-founded expectation of their domestic tranquillity. If, as Benedick asserts, they are both " too wise to woo peaceably," it may be added that both are too wise, too witty, and too wilful to live peaceably together. We have some misgivings about Beatrice—some apprehensions that poor Benedick will not escape the " predestinated scratched face," which he had foretold to him who should win and wear this quick-witted and pleasant-spirited lady; yet when we recollect that to the wit and imperious temper of Beatrice is united a magnanimity of spirit which would naturally place her far above all selfishness, and all paltry struggles for power—when we perceive, in the midst of her sarcastic levity and volubility of tongue, so much of generous affection, and such a high sense of female virtue and honour, we are inclined to hope the best. We think it possible that though the gentleman may now and then swear, and the lady scold, the native good-humour of the one, the really fine understanding of the other, and the value they so evidently attach to each other's esteem, will insure them a tolerable portion of domestic felicity; and in this hope we leave them.

NOTE BY THE EDITOR.—The poet Campbell, in his introduction to the play, remarks: "Mrs. Jameson, in her characters of Shakespeare, concludes with hoping that Beatrice will live happy with Benedick, but I have no such hope; and my final anticipation in reading the play is the certainty that Beatrice will provoke her Benedick to give her much and just conjugal castigation. She is an odious woman. Her own cousin says of her—

> 'Disdain and scorn ride sparkling in her eyes,
> Misprising what they look on, and her wit
> Values itself so highly that to her
> All matter else seems weak: she cannot love,
> Nor take no shape nor project of affection,
> She is so self-endeared.'

I once knew such a pair; the lady was a perfect Beatrice; she railed hypocritically at wedlock before her marriage, and with bitter sincerity after it. She and her Benedick now live apart, but with entire reciprocity of sentiments, each devoutly wishing that the other may soon pass into a better world. Beatrice is not to be compared, but contrasted, with Rosalind, who is equally witty; but the sparkling sayings of Rosalind are like gems upon her head at court, and like dew-drops on her bright hair in the woodland forest."

Verplanck, after quoting this passage, comments upon it as follows: "We extract this last criticism, partly in deference to Campbell's general exquisite taste and reverent appreciation of Shakespeare's genius, and partly as an example of the manner in which accidental personal associations influence taste and opinion. The critical poet seems to have unhappily suffered under the caprices or insolence of some accomplished but fantastical female wit, whose resemblance he thinks he recognizes in Beatrice; and then vents the offences of the belle of Edinburgh or London upon her prototype of Messina, or more probably of the court of Queen Elizabeth. Those who, without encountering any such unlucky cause of personal prejudice, have looked long enough upon the rapidly passing generations of wits and beauties in the gay world to have noted their characters as they first appeared, and subsequently developed themselves in after-life, will pronounce a very different judgment. Beatrice's faults are such as ordinarily spring from the consciousness of talent and beauty, accompanied with the high spirits of youth and health, and the play of a lively fancy. Her brilliant intellectual qualities are associated with strong and generous feelings, high confidence in female truth and virtue, warm attachment to her friends, and quick, undisguised indignation at wrong and injustice. There is the rich material, which the experience and the sorrows of maturer life, the affection and the duties of the wife and the mother, can gradually shape into the noblest forms of matronly excellence; and such, we doubt not, was the result shown in the married life of Beatrice."

We may add what Mr. Furnivall says on the same subject: "Beatrice is the sauciest, most piquant, sparkling, madcap girl that Shakspere ever drew, and yet a loving, deep-natured, true woman too.... She gives her heart to Benedick.... The two understand one another. We all know what it means. The brightest, sunniest married life, comfort in sorrow, doubling of joy.... The poet Campbell's story of his pair was an utter mistake: he never knew a Beatrice."

See also the extract from Gervinus, p. 18 above.

[*From Weiss's "Wit, Humor, and Shakspeare."**]

At first it seems as if Shakspeare intended by the introduction of Dogberry and his ineffective watch merely to interpolate a bit of comic business, by parodying the important phrases and impotent exploits of the suburban constable. But Dogberry's mission extended farther than that, and is intimately woven with delightful unconsciousness on his part into the fortunes of Hero.

Dogberry is not only immortal for that, but his name will never die so long as village communities in either hemi-

* *Wit, Humor, and Shakspeare*, by John Weiss (Boston, 1876), p. 75 fol.

sphere elect their guardians of the peace and clothe them in verbose terrors. If the town is unfortunately short of rascals, the officer will fear one in each bush, or extemporize one out of some unbelligerent starveling to show that the majestic instructions of his townsmen have not been wasted on him. This elaborate inefficiency is frequently selected by busy communities, because so few persons are there clumsy enough to be unemployed. Such a vagrom is easily comprehended. Dogberry has caught up the turns and idioms of sagacious speech, and seems to be blowing them up as life-belts; so he goes bobbing helplessly around in the froth of his talk. . . . He is the most original of Malaprops, says to the prince's order that it shall be suffigance, and tells the watch that salvation were a punishment too good for them, if they should have any allegiance in them. He has furnished mankind with that adroit phrase of conversational escape from compromise, "comparisons are odorous." . . . His brain seems to be web-footed, and tumbles over itself in trying to reach swimming-water; as when he says, "Masters, it is proved already that you are little better than false knaves, and it will go near to be thought so shortly." This is the precipitancy of a child's reasoning. . . .

Dogberry admires and cossets his own authority, but is too timid to enforce it save with poor old Verges, whose mental feebleness is an exact shadow of Dogberry's; and the latter manages to step upon himself in amusing unconsciousness. "An old man, sir, and his wits are not so blunt as, God help, I would desire they were." A good old man, sir, but he will gabble. All men are not alike, alas! So he goes on, dismissing himself, and slamming to the door without observing it.

But when the watch blunders by reason of idiocy into arresting Borachio, who was the agent in the plot against Hero, the innocent Conrade is found in his company, listening to his disclosures. He too is carried off and confronted with

Dogberry before the whole "dissembly" of constables. Then and there Conrade calls him in set terms an ass.

Dogberry flickers up into a kind of lukewarmness, and does his little to resent it. "Dost thou not suspect my years?" "Thou villain, thou art full of piety, as shall be proved." . . . He was never called ass before; for Conrade was probably the first free-spoken prisoner entirely innocent of malapropisms that he had ever faced. He cannot compose his shallow fluster; for it is as deep as he is, and it even comes splashing into the pathos of the moment when the wrong done to Hero is discovered, who is not yet known to be still living. He wants the man punished who called him ass, not the man who was the slanderer of Hero. Standing round him are noble natures touched with sorrow and remorse; but for him Conrade is "the plaintiff, the offender," who did call him ass. Dead, shamed, ruined Hero, distracted lover, and tender father retreat into a background upon which he scrawls himself an ass. . . . Here the comedy of Dogberry's character acquires a touch of humour; for so are we obliged to tolerate in our profoundest moments the trivialities of those who do not know or cannot contain our serious mood.

There is underlying humour in the fact that all this ignorance and inconsequence, this burlesquing of the detective's business, effects what the age and wisdom of Leonato and the instinct of the lover Claudio could not: namely, the discovery of Hero's innocence and of the plot to besmirch her chastity in the eyes of her lover. The wise men are taken in, and the accident of folly undeceives them. Then it becomes no longer an accident, but the regimen of the world adopts and puts it to a use. Here comedy becomes humorous, because it is shown how the fortunes of the good and prudent are involved with all the vulgarities of the world, and justice itself, which is nothing if not critical, cannot make up its case without *non-sequiturs*.

MUCH ADO ABOUT NOTHING.

DRAMATIS PERSONÆ

DON PEDRO, prince of Arragon.
DON JOHN, his bastard brother.
CLAUDIO, a young lord of Florence.
BENEDICK, a young lord of Padua.
LEONATO, governor of Messina.
ANTONIO, his brother.
BALTHAZAR, attendant on Don Pedro.
CONRADE, }
BORACHIO, } followers of Don John.
FRIAR FRANCIS.
DOGBERRY, a constable.
VERGES, a headborough.
A Sexton.
A Boy.

HERO, daughter to Leonato.
BEATRICE, niece to Leonato.
MARGARET, }
URSULA,   } gentlewomen attending on Hero.

Messengers, Watch, Attendants, &c.

SCENE: *Messina.*

ACT I.

Scene I. *Before Leonato's House.*

Enter Leonato, Hero, *and* Beatrice, *with a* Messenger.

Leonato. I learn in this letter that Don Pedro of Arragon comes this night to Messina.

Messenger. He is very near by this; he was not three leagues off when I left him.

Leonato. How many gentlemen have you lost in this action?

Messenger. But few of any sort, and none of name.

Leonato. A victory is twice itself when the achiever brings home full numbers. I find here that Don Pedro hath bestowed much honour on a young Florentine called Claudio.

Messenger. Much deserved on his part and equally remembered by Don Pedro; he hath borne himself beyond the promise of his age, doing in the figure of a lamb the feats of a lion: he hath indeed better bettered expectation than you must expect of me to tell you how.

Leonato. He hath an uncle here in Messina will be very much glad of it.

Messenger. I have already delivered him letters, and there appears much joy in him; even so much that joy could not show itself modest enough without a badge of bitterness.

Leonato. Did he break out into tears?

Messenger. In great measure.

Leonato. A kind overflow of kindness; there are no faces truer than those that are so washed. How much better is it to weep at joy than to joy at weeping!

Beatrice. I pray you, is Signior Montanto returned from the wars or no?

Messenger. I know none of that name, lady; there was none such in the army of any sort.

Leonato. What is he that you ask for, niece?

Hero. My cousin means Signior Benedick of Padua.

Messenger. O, he 's returned; and as pleasant as ever he was.

Beatrice. He set up his bills here in Messina and challenged Cupid at the flight; and my uncle's fool, reading the challenge, subscribed for Cupid, and challenged him at the bird bolt. I pray you, how many hath he killed and eaten in these wars? But how many hath he killed? for indeed I promised to eat all of his killing.

Leonato. Faith, niece, you tax Signior Benedick too much; but he 'll be meet with you, I doubt it not.

Messenger. He hath done good service, lady, in these wars.

Beatrice. You had musty victual, and he hath holp to eat it: he is a very valiant trencher-man; he hath an excellent stomach.

Messenger. And a good soldier too, lady.

Beatrice. And a good soldier to a lady; but what is he to a lord?

Messenger. A lord to a lord, a man to a man; stuffed with all honourable virtues. 50

Beatrice. It is so, indeed; he is no less than a stuffed man: but for the stuffing,—well, we are all mortal.

Leonato. You must not, sir, mistake my niece. There is a kind of merry war betwixt Signior Benedick and her; they never meet but there's a skirmish of wit between them.

Beatrice. Alas! he gets nothing by that. In our last conflict four of his five wits went halting off, and now is the whole man governed with one: so that if he have wit enough to keep himself warm, let him bear it for a difference between himself and his horse; for it is all the wealth that he hath left, to be known a reasonable creature.—Who is his companion now? He hath every month a new sworn brother.

Messenger. Is 't possible? 63

Beatrice. Very easily possible: he wears his faith but as the fashion of his hat; it ever changes with the next block.

Messenger. I see, lady, the gentleman is not in your books.

Beatrice. No; an he were, I would burn my study. But, I pray you, who is his companion? Is there no young squarer now that will make a voyage with him to the devil?

Messenger. He is most in the company of the right noble Claudio. 71

Beatrice. O Lord, he will hang upon him like a disease; he is sooner caught than the pestilence, and the taker runs presently mad. God help the noble Claudio! if he have caught the Benedick, it will cost him a thousand pound ere he be cured.

Messenger. I will hold friends with you, lady.

Beatrice. Do, good friend.

Leonato. You will never run mad, niece.

Beatrice. No, not till a hot January. 80

Messenger. Don Pedro is approached.

Enter Don Pedro, Don John, Claudio, Benedick, *and* Balthazar.

Don Pedro. Good Signior Leonato, you are come to meet your trouble; the fashion of the world is to avoid cost, and you encounter it.

Leonato. Never came trouble to my house in the likeness of your grace: for trouble being gone, comfort should remain; but when you depart from me, sorrow abides and happiness takes his leave.

Don Pedro. You embrace your charge too willingly. I think this is your daughter. 90

Leonato. Her mother hath many times told me so.

Benedick. Were you in doubt, sir, that you asked her?

Leonato. Signior Benedick, no; for then were you a child.

Don Pedro. You have it full, Benedick; we may guess by this what you are, being a man. Truly, the lady fathers herself.—Be happy, lady; for you are like an honourable father.

Benedick. If Signior Leonato be her father, she would not have his head on her shoulders for all Messina, as like him as she is. 100

Beatrice. I wonder that you will still be talking, Signior Benedick: nobody marks you.

Benedick. What, my dear Lady Disdain! are you yet living?

Beatrice. Is it possible disdain should die while she hath such meet food to feed it as Signior Benedick? Courtesy itself must convert to disdain, if you come in her presence.

Benedick. Then is courtesy a turncoat. But it is certain I am loved of all ladies, only you excepted: and I would I could find in my heart that I had not a hard heart; for, truly, I love none. 111

Beatrice. A dear happiness to women; they would else have been troubled with a pernicious suitor. I thank God and my cold blood, I am of your humour for that; I had rather hear my dog bark at a crow than a man swear he loves me.

Benedick. God keep your ladyship still in that mind! so some gentleman or other shall scape a predestinate scratched face.

Beatrice. Scratching could not make it worse, an 't were such a face as yours were.

Benedick. Well, you are a rare parrot-teacher.

Beatrice. A bird of my tongue is better than a beast of yours.

Benedick. I would my horse had the speed of your tongue, and so good a continuer. But keep your way, o' God's name; I have done.

Beatrice. You always end with a jade's trick; I know you of old.

Don Pedro. That is the sum of all, Leonato.— Signior Claudio and Signior Benedick, my dear friend Leonato hath invited you all. I tell him we shall stay here at the least a month; and he heartily prays some occasion may detain us longer. I dare swear he is no hypocrite, but prays from his heart.

Leonato. If you swear, my lord, you shall not be forsworn. —[*To Don John*] Let me bid you welcome, my lord: being reconciled to the prince your brother, I owe you all duty.

Don John. I thank you; I am not of many words, but I thank you.

Leonato. Please it your grace lead on?

Don Pedro. Your hand, Leonato; we will go together.

[*Exeunt all except Benedick and Claudio.*

Claudio. Benedick, didst thou note the daughter of Signior Leonato?

Benedick. I noted her not; but I looked on her.

Claudio. Is she not a modest young lady?

Benedick. Do you question me, as an honest man should

do, for my simple true judgment; or would you have me speak after my custom, as being a professed tyrant to their sex?   150

Claudio. No; I pray thee speak in sober judgment.

Benedick. Why, i' faith, methinks she 's too low for a high praise, too brown for a fair praise, and too little for a great praise: only this commendation I can afford her, that were she other than she is, she were unhandsome; and being no other but as she is, I do not like her.

Claudio. Thou thinkest I am in sport; I pray thee tell me truly how thou likest her.

Benedick. Would you buy her, that you inquire after her?

Claudio. Can the world buy such a jewel?   160

Benedick. Yea, and a case to put it into. But speak you this with a sad brow? or do you play the flouting Jack, to tell us Cupid is a good hare-finder and Vulcan a rare carpenter? Come, in what key shall a man take you, to go in the song?

Claudio. In mine eye she is the sweetest lady that ever I looked on.

Benedick. I can see yet without spectacles, and I see no such matter; there 's her cousin, an she were not possessed with a fury, exceeds her as much in beauty as the first of May doth the last of December. But I hope you have no intent to turn husband, have you?   172

Claudio. I would scarce trust myself, though I had sworn the contrary, if Hero would be my wife.

Benedick. Is 't come to this, i' faith? Hath not the world one man but he will wear his cap with suspicion? Shall I never see a bachelor of threescore again? Go to, i' faith; an thou wilt needs thrust thy neck into a yoke, wear the print of it and sigh away Sundays. Look, Don Pedro is returned to seek you.

Re-enter DON PEDRO.

Don Pedro. What secret hath held you here, that you followed not to Leonato's? 181

Benedick. I would your grace would constrain me to tell.

Don Pedro. I charge thee on thy allegiance.

Benedick. You hear, Count Claudio: I can be secret as a dumb man, I would have you think so; but, on my allegiance, mark you this, on my allegiance. — He is in love. With who? now that is your grace's part. Mark how short his answer is:—With Hero, Leonato's short daughter.

Claudio. If this were so, so were it uttered.

Benedick. Like the old tale, my lord: 'it is not so, nor 't was not so, but, indeed, God forbid it should be so.' 191

Claudio. If my passion change not shortly, God forbid it should be otherwise.

Don Pedro. Amen, if you love her; for the lady is very well worthy.

Claudio. You speak this to fetch me in, my lord.

Don Pedro. By my troth, I speak my thought.

Claudio. And, in faith, my lord, I spoke mine.

Benedick. And, by my two faiths and troths, my lord, I spoke mine. 200

Claudio. That I love her, I feel.

Don Pedro. That she is worthy, I know.

Benedick. That I neither feel how she should be loved nor know how she should be worthy, is the opinion that fire cannot melt out of me; I will die in it at the stake.

Don Pedro. Thou wast ever an obstinate heretic in the despite of beauty.

Claudio. And never could maintain his part but in the force of his will. 209

Benedick. That a woman conceived me, I thank her; that she brought me up, I likewise give her most humble thanks: but that I will have a recheat winded in my forehead, or hang my bugle in an invisible baldrick, all women shall pardon me. Because I will not do them the wrong to mistrust any, I will do myself the right to trust none; and the fine is, for the which I may go the finer, I will live a bachelor.

Don Pedro. I shall see thee, ere I die, look pale with love. 218

Benedick. With anger, with sickness, or with hunger, my lord, not with love; prove that ever I lose more blood with love than I will get again with drinking, pick out mine eyes with a ballad-maker's pen and hang me up at the door of a brothel-house for the sign of blind Cupid.

Don Pedro. Well, if ever thou dost fall from this faith, thou wilt prove a notable argument.

Benedick. If I do, hang me in a bottle like a cat and shoot at me; and he that hits me, let him be clapped on the shoulder, and called Adam.

Don Pedro. Well, as time shall try;
'In time the savage bull doth bear the yoke.' 230

Benedick. The savage bull may, but if ever the sensible Benedick bear it, pluck off the bull's horns and set them in my forehead; and let me be vilely painted, and in such great letters as they write 'Here is good horse to hire,' let them signify under my sign 'Here you may see Benedick the married man.'

Claudio. If this should ever happen, thou wouldst be horn-mad.

Don Pedro. Nay, if Cupid have not spent all his quiver in Venice, thou wilt quake for this shortly. 240

Benedick. I look for an earthquake too, then.

Don Pedro. Well, you will temporize with the hours. In the meantime, good Signior Benedick, repair to Leonato's: commend me to him, and tell him I will not fail him at supper; for indeed he hath made great preparation.

Benedick. I have almost matter enough in me for such an message; and so I commit you—

ACT I. SCENE I.

Claudio. To the tuition of God: from my house, if I had it,— 249

Don Pedro. The sixth of July: your loving friend, Benedick.

Benedick. Nay, mock not, mock not. The body of your discourse is sometime guarded with fragments, and the guards are but slightly basted on neither: ere you flout old ends any further, examine your conscience; and so I leave you. [*Exit.*

Claudio. My liege, your highness now may do me good.

Don Pedro. My love is thine to teach; teach it but how,
And thou shalt see how apt it is to learn
Any hard lesson that may do thee good.

Claudio. Hath Leonato any son, my lord? 260

Don Pedro. No child but Hero; she's his only heir.
Dost thou affect her, Claudio?

Claudio. O, my lord,
When you went onward on this ended action,
I look'd upon her with a soldier's eye,
That lik'd, but had a rougher task in hand
Than to drive liking to the name of love;
But now I am return'd and that war-thoughts
Have left their places vacant, in their rooms
Come thronging soft and delicate desires,
All prompting me how fair young Hero is, 270
Saying, I lik'd her ere I went to wars,—

Don Pedro. Thou wilt be like a lover presently
And tire the hearer with a book of words.
If thou dost love fair Hero, cherish it,
And I will break with her and with her father,
And thou shalt have her. Was't not to this end
That thou began'st to twist so fine a story?

Claudio. How sweetly you do minister to love,
That know love's grief by his complexion!
But lest my liking might too sudden seem, 280
I would have salv'd it with a longer treatise.

Don Pedro. What need the bridge much broader than the
  flood?
The fairest grant is the necessity.
Look, what will serve is fit; 't is once, thou lovest,
And I will fit thee with the remedy.
I know we shall have revelling to-night;
I will assume thy part in some disguise
And tell fair Hero I am Claudio,
And in her bosom I 'll unclasp my heart
And take her hearing prisoner with the force 290
And strong encounter of my amorous tale:
Then after to her father will I break;
And the conclusion is, she shall be thine.
In practice let us put it presently.   [*Exeunt.*

Scene II. *A Room in Leonato's House.*

Enter Leonato *and* Antonio, *meeting.*

Leonato. How now, brother! Where is my cousin, your son? hath he provided this music?

Antonio. He is very busy about it. But, brother, I can tell you strange news that you yet dreamt not of.

Leonato. Are they good?

Antonio. As the event stamps them; but they have a good cover, they show well outward. The prince and Count Claudio, walking in a thick-pleached alley in mine orchard, were thus much overheard by a man of mine: the prince discovered to Claudio that he loved my niece your daughter and meant to acknowledge it this night in a dance; and if he found her accordant, he meant to take the present time by the top and instantly break with you of it. 13

Leonato. Hath the fellow any wit that told you this?

Antonio. A good sharp fellow; I will send for him, and question him yourself.

Leonato. No, no; we will hold it as a dream till it appear itself: but I will acquaint my daughter withal, that she may be the better prepared for an answer, if peradventure this be true. Go you and tell her of it.—[*Enter attendants.*] Cousins, you know what you have to do.— O, I cry you mercy, friend; go you with me, and I will use your skill.— Good cousin, have a care this busy time. [*Exeunt.*

SCENE III. *The Same.*

Enter DON JOHN *and* CONRADE.

Conrade. What the good-year, my lord! why are you thus out of measure sad?

Don John. There is no measure in the occasion that breeds it; therefore the sadness is without limit.

Conrade. You should hear reason.

Don John. And when I have heard it, what blessing brings it?

Conrade. If not a present remedy, at least a patient sufferance. 9

Don John. I wonder that thou, being, as thou sayest thou art, born under Saturn, goest about to apply a moral medicine to a mortifying mischief. I cannot hide what I am; I must be sad when I have cause and smile at no man's jests, eat when I have stomach and wait for no man's leisure, sleep when I am drowsy and tend on no man's business, laugh when I am merry and claw no man in his humour. 16

Conrade. Yea, but you must not make the full show of this till you may do it without controlment. You have of late stood out against your brother, and he hath ta'en you newly into his grace, where it is impossible you should take true root but by the fair weather that you make yourself; it is needful that you frame the season for your own harvest.

Don John. I had rather be a canker in a hedge than a rose in his grace, and it better fits my blood to be disdained of all than to fashion a carriage to rob love from any; in

this, though I cannot be said to be a flattering honest man,
it must not be denied but I am a plain-dealing villain. I
am trusted with a muzzle and enfranchised with a clog;
therefore I have decreed not to sing in my cage. If I had
my mouth, I would bite; if I had my liberty, I would do my
liking: in the mean time let me be that I am and seek
not to alter me.

Conrade. Can you make no use of your discontent?

Don John. I make all use of it, for I use it only.—Who
comes here?—

Enter BORACHIO.

What news, Borachio?

Borachio. I came yonder from a great supper: the prince
your brother is royally entertained by Leonato; and I can
give you intelligence of an intended marriage.

Don John. Will it serve for any model to build mischief
on? What is he for a fool that betroths himself to unquiet-
ness?

Borachio. Marry, it is your brother's right hand.

Don John. Who? the most exquisite Claudio?

Borachio. Even he.

Don John. A proper squire! And who, and who? which
way looks he?

Borachio. Marry, on Hero, the daughter and heir of Leonato.

Don John. A very forward March-chick! How came
you to this?

Borachio. Being entertained for a perfumer, as I was smoking a musty room, comes me the prince and Claudio, hand
in hand, in sad conference; I whipt me behind the arras,
and there heard it agreed upon that the prince should woo
Hero for himself, and having obtained her, give her to Count
Claudio.

Don John. Come, come, let us thither; this may prove

food to my displeasure. That young start-up hath all the glory of my overthrow; if I can cross him any way, I bless myself every way. You are both sure, and will assist me?

Conrade. To the death, my lord. 62

Don John. Let us to the great supper; their cheer is the greater that I am subdued. Would the cook were of my mind! Shall we go prove what's to be done?

Borachio. We'll wait upon your lordship. [*Exeunt.*

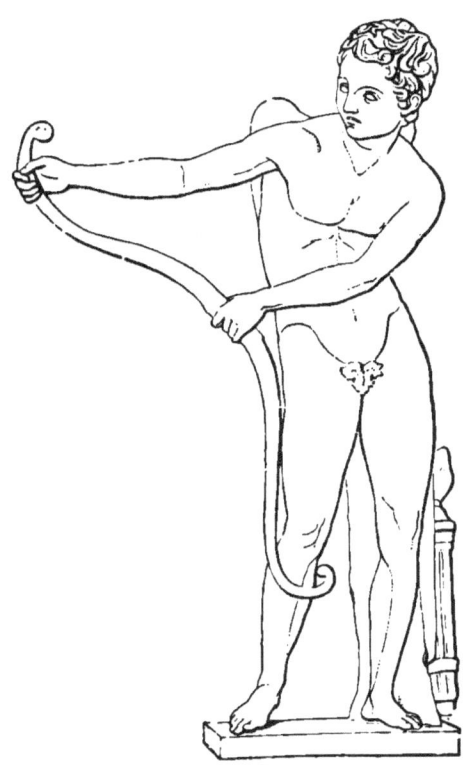

"the little hangman" (iii. 2. 10).

ACT II.

Scene I. *A Hall in* Leonato's *House.*

Enter Leonato, Antonio, Hero, Beatrice, *and others.*

Leonato. Was not Count John here at supper?
Antonio. I saw him not.
Beatrice. How tartly that gentleman looks! I never can
  I'm but I am heart-burned an hour after.
  H   He is of a very melancholy disposition.

Beatrice. He were an excellent man that were made just in the midway between him and Benedick; the one is too like an image and says nothing, and the other too like my lady's eldest son, evermore tattling. 9

Leonato. Then half Signior Benedick's tongue in Count John's mouth, and half Count John's melancholy in Signior Benedick's face,—

Beatrice. With a good leg and a good foot, uncle, and money enough in his purse, such a man would win any woman in the world,—if he could get her good will.

Leonato. By my troth, niece, thou wilt never get thee a husband, if thou be so shrewd of thy tongue.

Antonio. In faith, she's too curst.

Beatrice. Too curst is more than curst: I shall lessen God's sending that way; for it is said, 'God sends a curst cow short horns;' but to a cow too curst he sends none. 21

Leonato. So, by being too curst, God will send you no horns.

Beatrice. Just, if he send me no husband; for the which blessing I am at him upon my knees every morning and evening. Lord! I could not endure a husband with a beard on his face; I had rather lie in the woollen.

Leonato. You may light on a husband that hath no beard.

Beatrice. What should I do with him? dress him in my apparel and make him my waiting-gentlewoman? He that hath a beard is more than a youth, and he that hath no beard is less than a man; and he that is more than a youth is not for me, and he that is less than a man I am not for him: therefore I will even take sixpence in earnest of the bear-herd, and lead his apes into hell. 35

Leonato. Well, then, go you into hell?

Beatrice. No, but to the gate; and there will the devil meet me, like an old cuckold, with horns on his head, and say 'Get you to heaven, Beatrice, get you to heaven; here's no place for you maids:' so deliver I up my apes, and away to Saint Peter for the heavens; he shows me where the bachelors sit, and there live we as merry as the day is long.

Antonio. [*To Hero*] Well, niece, I trust you will be ruled by your father.

Beatrice. Yes, faith; it is my cousin's duty to make curtsy and say 'Father, as it please you.'—But yet for all that, cousin, let him be a handsome fellow, or else make another curtsy and say 'Father, as it please me.'

Leonato. Well, niece, I hope to see you one day fitted with a husband.

Beatrice. Not till God make men of some other metal than earth. Would it not grieve a woman to be overmastered with a piece of valiant dust? to make an account of her life to a clod of wayward marl? No, uncle, I'll none: Adam's sons are my brethren; and, truly, I hold it a sin to match in my kindred.

Leonato. Daughter, remember what I told you; if the prince do solicit you in that kind, you know your answer.

Beatrice. The fault will be in the music, cousin, if you be not wooed in good time; if the prince be too important, tell him there is measure in every thing, and so dance out the answer. For, hear me, Hero; wooing, wedding, and repenting, is as a Scotch jig, a measure, and a cinque-pace: the first suit is hot and hasty, like a Scotch jig, and full as fantastical; the wedding, mannerly-modest, as a measure, full of state and ancientry; and then comes repentance, and with his bad legs falls into the cinque-pace faster and faster, till he sink into his grave.

Leonato. Cousin, you apprehend passing shrewdly.

Beatrice. I have a good eye, uncle; I can see a church by daylight.

Leonato. The revellers are entering, brother; make good room. [*All put on their masks.*

Enter Don Pedro, Claudio, Benedick, Balthazar, Don John, Borachio, Margaret, Ursula, *and others, masked.*

Don Pedro. Lady, will you walk about with your friend?

Hero. So you walk softly and look sweetly and say nothing, I am yours for the walk; and especially when I walk away.

Don Pedro. With me in your company?

Hero. I may say so, when I please.

Don Pedro. And when please you to say so? 80

Hero. When I like your favour; for God defend the lute should be like the case!

Don Pedro. My visor is Philemon's roof; within the house is Jove.

Hero. Why, then, your visor should be thatch'd.

Don Pedro.   Speak low, if you speak love.
             [*Drawing her aside.*

Balthazar. Well, I would you did like me.

Margaret. So would not I, for your own sake; for I have many ill qualities.

Balthazar. Which is one?

Margaret. I say my prayers aloud. 90

Balthazar. I love you the better; the hearers may cry Amen.

Margaret. God match me with a good dancer!

Balthazar. Amen.

Margaret. And God keep him out of my sight when the dance is done! Answer, clerk.

Balthazar. No more words; the clerk is answered.

Ursula. I know you well enough; you are Signior Antonio.

Antonio. At a word, I am not. 100

Ursula. I know you by the waggling of your head.

Antonio. To tell you true, I counterfeit him.

Ursula. You could never do him so ill-well, unless you

were the very man. Here 's his dry hand up and down; you are he, you are he.

Antonio. At a word, I am not.

Ursula. Come, come, do you think I do not know you by your excellent wit? can virtue hide itself? Go to, mum, you are he; graces will appear, and there 's an end.

Beatrice. Will you not tell me who told you so? 110

Benedick. No, you shall pardon me.

Beatrice. Nor will you not tell me who you are?

Benedick. Not now.

Beatrice. That I was disdainful, and that I had my good wit out of the 'Hundred Merry Tales:'—well, this was Signior Benedick that said so.

Benedick. What 's he?

Beatrice. I am sure you know him well enough.

Benedick. Not I, believe me.

Beatrice. Did he never make you laugh? 120

Benedick. I pray you, what is he?

Beatrice. Why, he is the prince's jester: a very dull fool; only his gift is in devising impossible slanders: none but libertines delight in him; and the commendation is not in his wit, but in his villany; for he both pleases men and angers them, and then they laugh at him and beat him. I am sure he is in the fleet; I would he had boarded me.

Benedick. When I know the gentleman, I 'll tell him what you say. 129

Beatrice. Do, do: he 'll but break a comparison or two on me; which, peradventure not marked or not laughed at, strikes him into melancholy; and then there 's a partridge wing saved, for the fool will eat no supper that night. [*Music.*] We must follow the leaders.

Benedick. In every good thing.

Beatrice. Nay, if they lead to any ill, I will leave them at the next turning.   [*Dance. Then exeunt all except Don John, Borachio, and Claudio.*

Don John. Sure my brother is amorous on Hero and hath withdrawn her father to break with him about it. The ladies follow her and but one visor remains. 140

Borachio. And that is Claudio; I know him by his bearing.

Don John. Are not you Signior Benedick?

Claudio. You know me well; I am he.

Don John. Signior, you are very near my brother in his love: he is enamoured on Hero; I pray you, dissuade him from her: she is no equal for his birth. You may do the part of an honest man in it.

Claudio. How know you he loves her?

Don John. I heard him swear his affection. 150

Borachio. So did I too; and he swore he would marry her to-night.

Don John. Come, let us to the banquet.

[*Exeunt Don John and Borachio.*

Claudio. Thus answer I in name of Benedick,
But hear these ill news with the ears of Claudio.
'T is certain so; the prince wooes for himself.
Friendship is constant in all other things
Save in the office and affairs of love:
Therefore all hearts in love use their own tongues;
Let every eye negotiate for itself 160
And trust no agent; for beauty is a witch
Against whose charms faith melteth into blood.
This is an accident of hourly proof,
Which I mistrusted not. Farewell, therefore, Hero!

Re-enter BENEDICK.

Benedick. Count Claudio?

Claudio. Yea, the same.

Benedick. Come, will you go with me?

Claudio. Whither? 165

Benedick. Even to the next willow, about your own business, county. What fashion will you wear the garland of? about your neck, like an usurer's chain? or under your arm, like a lieutenant's scarf? You must wear it one way, for the prince hath got your Hero.

Claudio. I wish him joy of her.

Benedick. Why, that 's spoken like an honest drovier; so they sell bullocks. But did you think the prince would have served you thus?

Claudio. I pray you, leave me.

Benedick. Ho! now you strike like the blind man; 't was the boy that stole your meat, and you 'll beat the post. 180

Claudio. If it will not be, I 'll leave you. [*Exit.*

Benedick. Alas, poor hurt fowl! now will he creep into sedges. But that my Lady Beatrice should know me, and not know me! The prince's fool! Ha? It may be I go under that title because I am merry. Yea, but so I am apt to do myself wrong; I am not so reputed: it is the base, though bitter disposition of Beatrice that puts the world into her person, and so gives me out. Well, I 'll be revenged as I may. 185

Re-enter DON PEDRO.

Don Pedro. Now, signior, where 's the count? did you see him?

Benedick. Troth, my lord, I have played the part of Lady Fame. I found him here as melancholy as a lodge in a warren: I told him, and I think I told him true, that your grace had got the good will of this young lady; and I offered him my company to a willow-tree, either to make him a garland, as being forsaken, or to bind him up a rod, as being worthy to be whipped.

Don Pedro. To be whipped! What 's his fault? 191

Benedick. The flat transgression of a school-boy, who, being overjoyed with finding a bird's nest, shows it his companion, and he steals it.

Don Pedro. Wilt thou make a trust a transgression? The transgression is in the stealer.

Benedick. Yet it had not been amiss the rod had been made, and the garland too; for the garland he might have worn himself, and the rod he might have bestowed on you, who, as I take it, have stolen his bird's nest.

Don Pedro. I will but teach them to sing, and restore them to the owner. 210

Benedick. If their singing answer your saying, by my faith, you say honestly.

Don Pedro. The Lady Beatrice hath a quarrel to you; the gentleman that danced with her told her she is much wronged by you.

Benedick. O, she misused me past the endurance of a block! an oak but with one green leaf on it would have answered her; my very visor began to assume life and scold with her. She told me, not thinking I had been myself, that I was the prince's jester, that I was duller than a great thaw; huddling jest upon jest with such impossible conveyance upon me that I stood like a man at a mark, with a whole army shooting at me. She speaks poniards, and every word stabs: if her breath were as terrible as her terminations, there were no living near her; she would infect to the north star. I would not marry her, though she were endowed with all that Adam had left him before he transgressed; she would have made Hercules have turned spit, yea, and have cleft his club to make the fire too. Come, talk not of her; you shall find her the infernal Ate in good apparel. I would to God some scholar would conjure her; for certainly, while she is here, a man may live as quiet in hell as in a sanctuary; and people sin upon purpose, because they would go thither: so, indeed, all disquiet, horror, and perturbation follows her. 235

Don Pedro Look, here she comes.

D

Enter CLAUDIO, BEATRICE, HERO, *and* LEONATO.

Benedick. Will your grace command me any service to the world's end? I will go on the slightest errand now to the Antipodes that you can devise to send me on; I will fetch you a toothpicker now from the furthest inch of Asia, bring you the length of Prester John's foot, fetch you a hair off the great Cham's beard, do you any embassage to the Pigmies, rather than hold three words' conference with this harpy. You have no employment for me? 244

Don Pedro. None, but to desire your good company.

Benedick. O God, sir, here's a dish I love not; I cannot endure my Lady Tongue. [*Exit.*

Don Pedro. Come, lady, come; you have lost the heart of Signior Benedick.

Beatrice. Indeed, my lord, he lent it me awhile; and I gave him use for it, a double heart for his single one: marry, once before he won it of me with false dice, therefore your grace may well say I have lost it.

Don Pedro. You have put him down, lady, you have put him down. 255

Beatrice. So I would not he should do me, my lord. I have brought Count Claudio, whom you sent me to seek.

Don Pedro. Why, how now, count! wherefore are you sad?

Claudio. Not sad, my lord.

Don Pedro. How then? sick?

Claudio. Neither, my lord.

Beatrice. The count is neither sad, nor sick, nor merry, nor well; but civil count, civil as an orange, and something of that jealous complexion.

Don Pedro. I' faith, lady, I think your blazon to be true; though, I'll be sworn, if he be so, his conceit is false.—Here, Claudio, I have wooed in thy name, and fair Hero is won; I have broke with her father, and his good will obtained: name the day of marriage, and God give thee joy! 269

Leonato. Count, take of me my daughter, and with her my fortunes; his grace hath made the match, and all grace say Amen to it!

Beatrice. Speak, count, 't is your cue.

Claudio. Silence is the perfectest herald of joy; I were but little happy, if I could say how much.—Lady, as you are mine, I am yours; I give away myself for you, and dote upon the exchange.

Beatrice. Speak, cousin; or, if you cannot, stop his mouth with a kiss, and let not him speak neither.

Don Pedro. In faith, lady, you have a merry heart. 280

Beatrice. Yea, my lord; I thank it, poor fool, it keeps on the windy side of care. My cousin tells him in his ear that he is in her heart.

Claudio. And so she doth, cousin.

Beatrice. Good Lord, for alliance!—Thus goes every one to the world but I, and I am sunburnt; I may sit in a corner and cry heigh-ho for a husband!

Don Pedro. Lady Beatrice, I will get you one. 288

Beatrice. I would rather have one of your father's getting. Hath your grace ne'er a brother like you? Your father got excellent husbands, if a maid could come by them.

Don Pedro. Will you have me, lady?

Beatrice. No, my lord, unless I might have another for working-days; your grace is too costly to wear every day. But, I beseech your grace, pardon me; I was born to speak all mirth and no matter.

Don Pedro. Your silence most offends me, and to be merry best becomes you; for, out of question, you were born in a merry hour. 299

Beatrice. No, sure, my lord, my mother cried; but then there was a star danced, and under that was I born.—Cousins, God give you joy!

Leonato. Niece, will you look to those things I told you of?

Beatrice. I cry you mercy, uncle.—By your grace's pardon.
[*Exit.*

Don Pedro. By my troth, a pleasant-spirited lady.

Leonato. There's little of the melancholy element in her, my lord: she is never sad but when she sleeps, and not ever sad then; for I have heard my daughter say, she hath often dreamed of unhappiness and waked herself with laughing.

Don Pedro. She cannot endure to hear tell of a husband.

Leonato. O, by no means; she mocks all her wooers out of suit.

Don Pedro. She were an excellent wife for Benedick.

Leonato. O Lord! my lord, if they were but a week married, they would talk themselves mad.

Don Pedro. County Claudio, when mean you to go to church?

Claudio. To-morrow, my lord; time goes on crutches till love have all his rites.

Leonato. Not till Monday, my dear son, which is hence a just seven-night; and a time too brief, too, to have all things answer my mind.

Don Pedro. Come, you shake the head at so long a breathing; but, I warrant thee, Claudio, the time shall not go dully by us. I will in the interim undertake one of Hercules' labours; which is, to bring Signior Benedick and the Lady Beatrice into a mountain of affection the one with the other. I would fain have it a match, and I doubt not but to fashion it, if you three will but minister such assistance as I shall give you direction.

Leonato. My lord, I am for you, though it cost me ten nights' watchings.

Claudio. And I, my lord.

Don Pedro. And you too, gentle Hero?

Hero. I will do any modest office, my lord, to help my cousin to a good husband.

Don Pedro. And Benedick is not the unhopefullest husband that I know. Thus far can I praise him: he is of a noble strain, of approved valour and confirmed honesty. I will teach you how to humour your cousin, that she shall fall in love with Benedick; and I, with your two helps, will so practise on Benedick that, in despite of his quick wit and his queasy stomach, he shall fall in love with Beatrice. If we can do this, Cupid is no longer an archer; his glory shall be ours, for we are the only love-gods. Go in with me, and I will tell you my drift. [*Exeunt.*

SCENE II. *The Same.*

Enter DON JOHN *and* BORACHIO.

Don John. It is so; the Count Claudio shall marry the daughter of Leonato.

Borachio. Yea, my lord; but I can cross it.

Don John. Any bar, any cross, any impediment will be medicinable to me; I am sick in displeasure to him, and whatsoever comes athwart his affection ranges evenly with mine. How canst thou cross this marriage?

Borachio. Not honestly, my lord; but so covertly that no dishonesty shall appear in me.

Don John. Show me briefly how.

Borachio. I think I told your lordship, a year since, how much I am in the favour of Margaret, the waiting-gentlewoman to Hero.

Don John. I remember.

Borachio. I can, at any unseasonable instant of the night, appoint her to look out at her lady's chamber-window.

Don John. What life is in that, to be the death of this marriage?

Borachio. The poison of that lies in you to temper. Go you to the prince your brother; spare not to tell him that he hath wronged his honour in marrying the renowned Claudio —whose estimation do you mightily hold up—to a contaminated stale, such a one as Hero.

Don John. What proof shall I make of that?

Borachio. Proof enough to misuse the prince, to vex Claudio, to undo Hero, and kill Leonato. Look you for any other issue?

Don John. Only to despite them, I will endeavour any thing.   29

Borachio. Go, then; find me a meet hour to draw Don Pedro and Count Claudio alone: tell them that you know that Hero loves me; intend a kind of zeal both to the prince and Claudio, as—in love of your brother's honour, who hath made this match, and his friend's reputation, who is thus like to be cozened with the semblance of a maid—that you have discovered thus. They will scarcely believe this without trial: offer them instances; which shall bear no less likelihood than to see me at her chamber-window, hear me call Margaret Hero, hear Margaret term me Claudio; and bring them to see this the very night before the intended wedding, —for in the meantime I will so fashion the matter that Hero shall be absent,—and there shall appear such seeming truth of Hero's disloyalty that jealousy shall be called assurance and all the preparation overthrown.   44

Don John. Grow this to what adverse issue it can, I will put it in practice. Be cunning in the working this, and thy fee is a thousand ducats.

Borachio. Be you constant in the accusation, and my cunning shall not shame me.   49

Don John. I will presently go learn their day of marriage.
                                                 [*Exeunt.*

SCENE III. *Leonato's Orchard.*

Enter BENEDICK.

Benedick. Boy!

Enter Boy.

Boy. Signior?

Benedick. In my chamber-window lies a book; bring it hither to me in the orchard.

Boy. I am here already, sir.

Benedick. I know that; but I would have thee hence, and here again. [*Exit Boy.*] I do much wonder that one man, seeing how much another man is a fool when he dedicates his behaviours to love, will, after he hath laughed at such shallow follies in others, become the argument of his own scorn by falling in love; and such a man is Claudio. I have known when there was no music with him but the drum and the fife; and now had he rather hear the tabor and the pipe: I have known when he would have walked ten mile afoot to see a good armour; and now will he lie ten nights awake, carving the fashion of a new doublet. He was wont to speak plain and to the purpose, like an honest man and a soldier; and now is he turned orthography: his words are a very fantastical banquet, just so many strange dishes. May I be so converted and see with these eyes? I cannot tell; I think not. I will not be sworn but love may transform me to an oyster; but I'll take my oath on it, till he have made an oyster of me, he shall never make me such a fool. One woman is fair, yet I am well; another is wise, yet I am well; another virtuous, yet I am well; but till all graces be in one woman, one woman shall not come in my grace. Rich she shall be, that's certain; wise, or I'll none; virtuous, or I'll never cheapen her; fair, or I'll never look on her; mild, or come not near me; noble, or not I for an angel; of good discourse, an excellent musician, and her hair shall be of what colour it please God. Ha! the prince and Monsieur Love! I will hide me in the arbour.   [*Withdraws.*

Enter DON PEDRO, CLAUDIO, *and* LEONATO, *followed by* BALTHAZAR *and* Musicians.

Don Pedro. Come, shall we hear this music?

Claudio. Yea, my good lord. How still the evening is,
As hush'd on purpose to grace harmony!

Don Pedro. See you where Benedick hath hid himself?

Claudio. O, very well, my lord; the music ended,
We'll fit the kid-fox with a pennyworth.

Don Pedro. Come, Balthazar, we'll hear that song again.

Balthazar. O, good my lord, tax not so bad a voice 40
To slander music any more than once.

Don Pedro. It is the witness still of excellency
To put a strange face on his own perfection.
I pray thee, sing, and let me woo no more.

Balthazar. Because you talk of wooing, I will sing;
Since many a wooer doth commence his suit
To her he thinks not worthy; yet he wooes,
Yet will he swear he loves.

Don Pedro. Now, pray thee, come;
Or, if thou wilt hold longer argument,
Do it in notes.

Balthazar. Note this before my notes: 50
There's not a note of mine that's worth the noting.

Don Pedro. Why, these are very crotchets that he speaks;
Note, notes, forsooth, and nothing. [*Music.*

Benedick. Now, divine air! now is his soul ravished! Is it not strange that sheeps' guts should hale souls out of men's bodies? Well, a horn for my money, when all's done.

The Song.

Balthazar. *Sigh no more, ladies, sigh no more,*
 Men were deceivers ever,
One foot in sea and one on shore,
 To one thing constant never; 60
Then sigh not so, but let them go,
 And be you blithe and bonny,
Converting all your sounds of woe
 Into Hey nonny, nonny.

Sing no more ditties, sing no moe,
   Of dumps so dull and heavy;
The fraud of men was ever so,
   Since summer first was leavy:
Then sigh not so, etc.

Don Pedro. By my troth, a good song.

Balthazar. And an ill singer, my lord.

Don Pedro. Ha, no, no, faith; thou singest well enough for a shift.

Benedick. An he had been a dog that should have howled thus, they would have hanged him; and I pray God his bad voice bode no mischief! I had as lief have heard the night-raven, come what plague could have come after it.

Don Pedro. Yea, marry, dost thou hear, Balthazar? I pray thee, get us some excellent music; for to-morrow night we would have it at the Lady Hero's chamber-window.

Balthazar. The best I can, my lord.

Don Pedro. Do so; farewell. [*Exit Balthazar.*] Come hither, Leonato. What was it you told me of to-day, that your niece Beatrice was in love with Signior Benedick?

Claudio. O, ay: stalk on, stalk on; the fowl sits.—I did never think that lady would have loved any man.

Leonato. No, nor I neither; but most wonderful that she should so dote on Signior Benedick, whom she hath in all outward behaviours seemed ever to abhor.

Benedick. Is 't possible? Sits the wind in that corner?

Leonato. By my troth, my lord, I cannot tell what to think of it but that she loves him with an enraged affection: it is past the infinite of thought.

Don Pedro. May be she doth but counterfeit.

Claudio. Faith, like enough.

Leonato. O God, counterfeit! There was never counterfeit of passion came so near the life of passion as she discovers it.

Don Pedro. Why, what effects of passion shows she?

Claudio. Bait the hook well; this fish will bite.

Leonato. What effects, my lord? She will sit you, you heard my daughter tell you how.

Claudio. She did, indeed.

Don Pedro. How, how, I pray you? You amaze me; I would have thought her spirit had been invincible against all assaults of affection.

Leonato. I would have sworn it had, my lord; especially against Benedick.

Benedick. I should think this a gull, but that the white-bearded fellow speaks it; knavery cannot, sure, hide himself in such reverence.

Claudio. He hath ta'en the infection; hold it up.

Don Pedro. Hath she made her affection known to Benedick?

Leonato. No, and swears she never will; that's her torment.

Claudio. 'T is true, indeed; so your daughter says: 'Shall I,' says she, 'that have so oft encountered him with scorn, write to him that I love him?'

Leonato. This says she now when she is beginning to write to him; for she 'll be up twenty times a night, and there will she sit in her smock till she have writ a sheet of paper: my daughter tells us all.

Claudio. Now you talk of a sheet of paper, I remember a pretty jest your daughter told us of.

Leonato. O, when she had writ it and was reading it over, she found Benedick and Beatrice between the sheet?

Claudio. That.

Leonato. O, she tore the letter into a thousand halfpence; railed at herself, that she should be so immodest to write to one that she knew would flout her: 'I measure him,' says she, 'by my own spirit: for I should flout him, if he writ to me, yea, though I love him, I should.'

Claudio. Then down upon her knees she falls, weeps,

sobs, beats her heart, tears her hair, prays, cries, 'O sweet Benedick! God give me patience!'

Leonato. She doth indeed; my daughter says so: and the ecstasy hath so much overborne her that my daughter is sometime afeard she will do a desperate outrage to herself; it is very true. 140

Don Pedro. It were good that Benedick knew of it by some other, if she will not discover it.

Claudio. To what end? He would but make a sport of it and torment the poor lady worse.

Don Pedro. An he should, it were an alms to hang him. She's an excellent sweet lady; and, out of all suspicion, she is virtuous.

Claudio. And she is exceeding wise.

Don Pedro. In every thing but in loving Benedick. 149

Leonato. O, my lord, wisdom and blood combating in so tender a body, we have ten proofs to one that blood hath the victory. I am sorry for her, as I have just cause, being her uncle and her guardian.

Don Pedro. I would she had bestowed this dotage on me; I would have daffed all other respects and made her half myself. I pray you, tell Benedick of it, and hear what he will say.

Leonato. Were it good, think you?

Claudio. Hero thinks surely she will die; for she says she will die if he love her not, and she will die ere she make her love known, and she will die, if he woo her, rather than she will bate one breath of her accustomed crossness. 162

Don Pedro. She doth well: if she should make tender of her love, 't is very possible he 'll scorn it; for the man, as you know all, hath a contemptible spirit.

Claudio. He is a very proper man.

Don Pedro. He hath indeed a good outward happiness.

Claudio. Fore God, and, in my mind, very wise.

Don Pedro. He doth indeed show some sparks that are like wit.

Leonato. And I take him to be valiant.

Don Pedro. As Hector, I assure you: and in the managing of quarrels you may say he is wise; for either he avoids them with great discretion, or undertakes them with a most Christian-like fear.

Leonato. If he do fear God, he must necessarily keep peace; if he break the peace, he ought to enter into a quarrel with fear and trembling.

Don Pedro. And so will he do; for the man doth fear God, howsoever it seems not in him by some large jests he will make. Well, I am sorry for your niece. Shall we go seek Benedick, and tell him of her love?

Claudio. Never tell him, my lord; let her wear it out with good counsel.

Leonato. Nay, that's impossible; she may wear her heart out first.

Don Pedro. Well, we will hear further of it by your daughter; let it cool the while. I love Benedick well; and I could wish he would modestly examine himself, to see how much he is unworthy so good a lady.

Leonato. My lord, will you walk? dinner is ready.

Claudio. If he do not dote on her upon this, I will never trust my expectation.

Don Pedro. Let there be the same net spread for her; and that must your daughter and her gentlewoman carry. The sport will be, when they hold one an opinion of another's dotage, and no such matter; that's the scene that I would see, which will be merely a dumb-show. Let us send her to call him in to dinner.

[*Exeunt Don Pedro, Claudio, and Leonato.*

Benedick. [*Coming forward*] This can be no trick; the conference was sadly borne. They have the truth of this from Hero. They seem to pity the lady; it seems her affections have their full bent. Love me! why, it must be requited. I hear how I am censured: they say I will bear myself proudly, if I perceive the love come from her; they say too that she will rather die than give any sign of affection. I did never think to marry: I must not seem proud; happy are they that hear their detractions and can put them to mending. They say the lady is fair; 't is a truth, I can bear them witness: and virtuous; 't is so, I cannot reprove it: and wise, but for loving me; by my troth, it is no addition to her wit, nor no great argument of her folly, for I will be horribly in love with her. I may chance have some odd quirks and remnants of wit broken on me, because I have railed so long against marriage; but doth not the appetite alter? a man loves the meat in his youth that he cannot endure in his age. Shall quips and sentences and these paper bullets of the brain awe a man from the career of his humour? No, the world must be peopled. When I said I would die a bachelor, I did not think I should live till I were married.—Here comes Beatrice. By this day, she 's a fair lady; I do spy some marks of love in her. 223

Enter BEATRICE.

Beatrice. Against my will I am sent to bid you come in to dinner.

Benedick. Fair Beatrice, I thank you for your pains.

Beatrice. I took no more pains for those thanks than you take pains to thank me; if it had been painful, I would not have come.

Benedick. You take pleasure then in the message? 230

Beatrice. Yea, just so much as you may take upon a knife's point and choke a daw withal.—You have no stomach, signior; fare you well. [*Exit.*

Benedick. Ha! 'Against my will I am sent to bid you come in to dinner;' there 's a double meaning in that. 'I took no more pains for those thanks than you took pains to

62　*MUCH ADO ABOUT NOTHING.*

thank me;' that's as much as to say, Any pains that I take for you is as easy as thanks. If I do not take pity of her, I am a villain; if I do not love her, I am a Jew. I will go get her picture.　　　　　　　　　　　　　　　　　　*[Exit*

"haggards of the rock" (iii. 1. 36).

ACT III.

Scene I. *Leonato's Orchard.*

Enter Hero, Margaret, *and* Ursula.

Hero. Good Margaret, run thee to the parlour;
There shalt thou find my cousin Beatrice
Proposing with the prince and Claudio:
Whisper her ear and tell her, I and Ursula

Walk in the orchard and our whole discourse
Is all of her; say that thou overheard'st us;
And bid her steal into the pleached bower,
Where honeysuckles, ripen'd by the sun,
Forbid the sun to enter, like favourites,
Made proud by princes, that advance their pride   10
Against that power that bred it: there will she hide her,
To listen our propose. This is thy office;
Bear thee well in it, and leave us alone.
   Margaret. I'll make her come, I warrant you, presently.
                                                                              [*Exit.*
   Hero. Now, Ursula, when Beatrice doth come,
As we do trace this alley up and down,
Our talk must only be of Benedick.
When I do name him, let it be thy part
To praise him more than ever man did merit;
My talk to thee must be how Benedick   20
Is sick in love with Beatrice. Of this matter
Is little Cupid's crafty arrow made,
That only wounds by hearsay.

           Enter BEATRICE, *behind.*

                       Now begin;
For look where Beatrice, like a lapwing, runs
Close by the ground, to hear our conference.
   Ursula. The pleasant'st angling is to see the fish
Cut with her golden oars the silver stream,
And greedily devour the treacherous bait;
So angle we for Beatrice, who even now
Is couched in the woodbine coverture.   30
Fear you not my part of the dialogue.
   Hero. Then go we near her, that her ear lose nothing
Of the false sweet bait that we lay for it.
                                 [*Approaching the bower.*
No, truly, Ursula, she is too disdainful;

I know her spirits are as coy and wild
As haggards of the rock.
 Ursula.   But are you sure
That Benedick loves Beatrice so entirely?
 Hero. So says the prince and my new-trothed lord.
 Ursula. And did they bid you tell her of it, madam?
 Hero. They did entreat me to acquaint her of it; 40
But I persuaded them, if they lov'd Benedick,
To wish him wrestle with affection,
And never to let Beatrice know of it.
 Ursula. Why did you so? Doth not the gentleman
Deserve as full as fortunate a bed
As ever Beatrice shall couch upon?
 Hero. O god of love! I know he doth deserve
As much as may be yielded to a man:
But Nature never fram'd a woman's heart
Of prouder stuff than that of Beatrice; 50
Disdain and scorn ride sparkling in her eyes,
Misprising what they look on, and her wit
Values itself so highly that to her
All matter else seems weak: she cannot love,
Nor take no shape nor project of affection,
She is so self-endeared.
 Ursula.   Sure, I think so;
And therefore certainly it were not good
She knew his love, lest she make sport at it.
 Hero. Why, you speak truth. I never yet saw man,
How wise, how noble, young, how rarely featur'd, 60
But she would spell him backward: if fair-fac'd,
She would swear the gentleman should be her sister;
If black, why, Nature, drawing of an antic,
Made a foul blot; if tall, a lance ill-headed;
If low, an agate very vilely cut;
If speaking, why, a vane blown with all winds;
If silent, why, a block moved with none.

So turns she every man the wrong side out,
And never gives to truth and virtue that
Which simpleness and merit purchaseth. 70
 Ursula. Sure, sure, such carping is not commendable.
 Hero. No, not to be so odd and from all fashions
As Beatrice is, cannot be commendable;
But who dare tell her so? If I should speak,
She would mock me into air; O, she would laugh me
Out of myself, press me to death with wit.
Therefore let Benedick, like cover'd fire,
Consume away in sighs, waste inwardly;
It were a better death than die with mocks,
Which is as bad as die with tickling. 80
 Ursula. Yet tell her of it; hear what she will say.
 Hero. No; rather I will go to Benedick
And counsel him to fight against his passion.
And, truly, I'll devise some honest slanders
To stain my cousin with; one doth not know
How much an ill word may empoison liking.
 Ursula. O, do not do your cousin such a wrong.
She cannot be so much without true judgment—
Having so swift and excellent a wit
As she is priz'd to have—as to refuse 90
So rare a gentleman as Signior Benedick.
 Hero. He is the only man of Italy,
Always excepted my dear Claudio.
 Ursula. I pray you, be not angry with me, madam,
Speaking my fancy; Signior Benedick,
For shape, for bearing, argument, and valour,
Goes foremost in report through Italy.
 Hero. Indeed, he hath an excellent good name.
 Ursula. His excellence did earn it, ere he had it.
When are you married, madam? 100
 Hero. Why, every day, to-morrow. Come, go in;
I'll show thee some attires, and have thy counsel
Which is the best to furnish me to-morrow.

Ursula. She's lim'd, I warrant you; we have caught her, madam.

Hero. If it proves so, then loving goes by haps;
Some Cupid kills with arrows, some with traps.
                            [*Exeunt Hero and Ursula.*

Beatrice. [*Coming forward*] What fire is in mine ears?
    Can this be true?
Stand I condemn'd for pride and scorn so much?
Contempt, farewell! and maiden pride, adieu!
No glory lives behind the back of such.
And, Benedick, love on; I will requite thee,
    Taming my wild heart to thy loving hand:
If thou dost love, my kindness shall incite thee
    To bind our loves up in a holy band;
For others say thou dost deserve, and I
Believe it better than reportingly.   [*Exit.*

SCENE II. *A Room in Leonato's House.*

Enter DON PEDRO, CLAUDIO, BENEDICK, *and* LEONATO.

Don Pedro. I do but stay till your marriage be consummate, and then go I toward Arragon.

Claudio. I'll bring you thither, my lord, if you'll vouchsafe me.

Don Pedro. Nay, that would be as great a soil in the new gloss of your marriage as to show a child his new coat and forbid him to wear it. I will only be bold with Benedick for his company; for, from the crown of his head to the sole of his foot, he is all mirth: he hath twice or thrice cut Cupid's bow-string, and the little hangman dare not shoot at him. He hath a heart as sound as a bell and his tongue is the clapper, for what his heart thinks his tongue speaks.

Benedick. Gallants, I am not as I have been.

Leonato. So say I; methinks you are sadder.

Claudio. I hope he be in love.

Don Pedro. Hang him, truant! there's no true drop of blood in him, to be truly touched with love; if he be sad, he wants money.

Benedick. I have the toothache.

Don Pedro. Draw it.

Benedick. Hang it!

Claudio. You must hang it first, and draw it afterwards.

Don Pedro. What! sigh for the toothache?

Leonato. Where is but a humour or a worm?

Benedick. Well, every one can master a grief but he that has it.

Claudio. Yet say I, he is in love.

Don Pedro. There is no appearance of fancy in him, unless it be a fancy that he hath to strange disguises; as to be a Dutchman to-day, a Frenchman to-morrow, or in the shape of two countries at once, as a German from the waist downward, all slops, and a Spaniard from the hip upward, no doublet. Unless he have a fancy to this foolery, as it appears he hath, he is no fool for fancy, as you would have it appear he is.

Claudio. If he be not in love with some woman, there is no believing old signs: he brushes his hat o' mornings; what should that bode?

Don Pedro. Hath any man seen him at the barber's?

Claudio. No, but the barber's man hath been seen with him, and the old ornament of his cheek hath already stuffed tennis-balls.

Leonato. Indeed, he looks younger than he did, by the loss of a beard.

Don Pedro. Nay, he rubs himself with civet; can you smell him out by that?

Claudio. That's as much as to say, the sweet youth's in love.

Don Pedro. The greatest note of it is his melancholy.

Claudio. And when was he wont to wash his face?

Don Pedro. Yea, or to paint himself? for the which, I hear what they say of him.

Claudio. Nay, but his jesting spirit, which is now crept into a lute-string and now governed by stops.

Don Pedro. Indeed, that tells a heavy tale for him; conclude, conclude he is in love.

Claudio. Nay, but I know who loves him.

Don Pedro. That would I know too; I warrant, one that knows him not.

Claudio. Yes, and his ill conditions; and, in despite of all, dies for him.

Don Pedro. She shall be buried with her face upwards.

Benedick. Yet is this no charm for the toothache.—Old signior, walk aside with me; I have studied eight or nine wise words to speak to you, which these hobby-horses must not hear. [*Exeunt Benedick and Leonato.*

Don Pedro. For my life, to break with him about Beatrice.

Claudio. 'T is even so. Hero and Margaret have by this played their parts with Beatrice; and then the two bears will not bite one another when they meet.

Enter DON JOHN.

Don John. My lord and brother, God save you!

Don Pedro. Good den, brother.

Don John. If your leisure served, I would speak with you.

Don Pedro. In private?

Don John. If it please you: yet Count Claudio may hear; for what I would speak of concerns him.

Don Pedro. What 's the matter?

Don John. [*To Claudio*] Means your lordship to be married to-morrow?

Don Pedro. You know he does.

Don John. I know not that, when he knows what I know.

Claudio. If there be any impediment, I pray you discover it.

Don John. You may think I love you not; let that appear hereafter, and aim better at me by that I now will manifest. For my brother, I think he holds you well, and in dearness of heart hath holp to effect your ensuing marriage,—surely suit ill spent and labour ill bestowed.

Don Pedro. Why, what's the matter?

Don John. I came hither to tell you; and, circumstances shortened, for she has been too long a talking of, the lady is disloyal.

Claudio. Who? Hero?

Don John. Even she; Leonato's Hero, your Hero, every man's Hero.

Claudio. Disloyal?

Don John. The word is too good to paint out her wickedness; I could say she were worse: think you of a worse title, and I will fit her to it. Wonder not till further warrant; go but with me to-night, you shall see her chamber-window entered, even the night before her wedding-day: if you love her then, to-morrow wed her; but it would better fit your honour to change your mind.

Claudio. May this be so?

Don Pedro. I will not think it.

Don John. If you dare not trust that you see, confess not that you know: if you will follow me, I will show you enough; and when you have seen more and heard more, proceed accordingly.

Claudio. If I see any thing to-night why I should not marry her to-morrow, in the congregation, where I should wed, there will I shame her.

Don Pedro. And, as I wooed for thee to obtain her, I will join with thee to disgrace her.

Don John. I will disparage her no farther till you are my witnesses; bear it coldly but till midnight, and let the issue show itself.

Don Pedro. O day untowardly turned!

Claudio. O mischief strangely thwarting!

Don John. O plague right well prevented! so will you say when you have seen the sequel. [*Exeunt.*

Scene III. *A Street.*
Enter Dogberry *and* Verges *with the* Watch.

Dogberry. Are you good men and true?

Verges. Yea, or else it were pity but they should suffer salvation, body and soul.

Dogberry. Nay, that were a punishment too good for them, if they should have any allegiance in them, being chosen for the prince's watch.

Verges. Well, give them their charge, neighbour Dogberry.

Dogberry. First, who think you the most desartless man to be constable?

1 *Watch.* Hugh Oatcake, sir, or George Seacole; for they can write and read.

Dogberry. Come hither, neighbour Seacole. God hath blessed you with a good name; to be a well-favoured man is the gift of fortune, but to write and read comes by nature.

2 *Watch.* Both which, master constable,—

Dogberry. You have; I knew it would be your answer. Well, for your favour, sir, why, give God thanks, and make no boast of it; and for your writing and reading, let that appear when there is no need of such vanity. You are thought here to be the most senseless and fit man for the constable of the watch; therefore bear you the lantern. This is your charge: you shall comprehend all vagrom men; you are to bid any man stand, in the prince's name.

2 *Watch.* How if a' will not stand?

Dogberry. Why, then, take no note of him, but let him go; and presently call the rest of the watch together and thank God you are rid of a knave.

Verges. If he will not stand when he is bidden, he is none of the prince's subjects.

Dogberry. True, and they are to meddle with none but the prince's subjects.—You shall also make no noise in the streets; for for the watch to babble and to talk is most tolerable and not to be endured.

Watch. We will rather sleep than talk; we know what belongs to a watch.

Dogberry. Why, you speak like an ancient and most quiet watchman; for I cannot see how sleeping should offend: only, have a care that your bills be not stolen. Well, you are to call at all the ale-houses, and bid them that are drunk get them to bed.

Watch. How if they will not?

Dogberry. Why, then, let them alone till they are sober; if they make you not then the better answer, you may say they are not the men you took them for.

Watch. Well, sir.

Dogberry. If you meet a thief, you may suspect him, by virtue of your office, to be no true man; and, for such kind of men, the less you meddle or make with them, why, the more is for your honesty.

Watch. If we know him to be a thief, shall we not lay hands on him?

Dogberry. Truly, by your office, you may; but I think they that touch pitch will be defiled: the most peaceable way for you, if you do take a thief, is to let him show himself what he is and steal out of your company.

Verges. You have been always called a merciful man, partner.

Dogberry. Truly, I would not hang a dog by my will, much more a man who hath any honesty in him.

Verges. If you hear a child cry in the night, you must call to the nurse and bid her still it.

Watch. How if the nurse be asleep and will not hear us?

Dogberry Why, then, depart in peace, and let the child

wake her with crying; for the ewe that will not hear her lamb when it baes will never answer a calf when he bleats.

Verges. 'T is very true.

Dogberry. This is the end of the charge: you, constable, are to present the prince's own person; if you meet the prince in the night, you may stay him. 70

Verges. Nay, by 'r lady, that I think a' cannot.

Dogberry. Five shillings to one on 't, with any man that knows the statues, he may stay him : marry, not without the prince be willing; for, indeed, the watch ought to offend no man, and it is an offence to stay a man against his will.

Verges. By 'r lady, I think it be so.

Dogberry. Ha, ha, ha! Well, masters, good night. An there be any matter of weight chances, call up me : keep your fellows' counsels and your own; and good night. Come, neighbour. 80

Watch. Well, masters, we hear our charge; let us go sit here upon the church-bench till two, and then all to bed.

Dogberry. One word more, honest neighbours. I pray you, watch about Signior Leonato's door; for, the wedding being there to-morrow, there is a great coil to-night. Adieu; be vigitant, I beseech you. [*Exeunt Dogberry and Verges.*

Enter BORACHIO *and* CONRADE.

Borachio. What, Conrade!

Watch. [*Aside*] Peace! stir not.

Borachio. Conrade, I say!

Conrade. Here, man; I am at thy elbow. 90

Borachio. Mass, and my elbow itched; I thought there would a scab follow.

Conrade. I will owe thee an answer for that; and now forward with thy tale.

Borachio. Stand thee close, then, under this pent-house, for it drizzles rain; and I will, like a true drunkard, utter all to thee.

Watch. [*Aside*] Some treason, masters; yet stand close.

Borachio. Therefore know I have earned of Don John a thousand ducats. 100

Conrade. Is it possible that any villany should be so dear?

Borachio. Thou shouldst rather ask if it were possible any villany should be so rich; for when rich villains have need of poor ones, poor ones may make what price they will.

Conrade. I wonder at it.

Borachio. That shows thou art unconfirmed. Thou knowest that the fashion of a doublet, or a hat, or a cloak, is nothing to a man.

Conrade. Yes, it is apparel.

Borachio. I mean, the fashion. 110

Conrade. Yes, the fashion is the fashion.

Borachio. Tush! I may as well say the fool 's the fool. But seest thou not what a deformed thief this fashion is?

Watch. [*Aside*] I know that Deformed; a' has been a vile thief this seven year: a' goes up and down like a gentleman. I remember his name.

Borachio. Didst thou not hear somebody?

Conrade. No; 't was the vane on the house. 118

Borachio. Seest thou not, I say, what a deformed thief this fashion is? how giddily a' turns about all the hot bloods between fourteen and five-and-thirty? sometime fashioning them like Pharaoh's soldiers in the reechy painting, sometime like god Bel's priests in the old church-window, sometime like the shaven Hercules in the smirched worm-eaten tapestry.

Conrade. All this I see; and I see that the fashion wears out more apparel than the man. But art not thou thyself giddy with the fashion too, that thou hast shifted out of thy tale into telling me of the fashion? 129

Borachio. Not so, neither: but know that I have to-night wooed Margaret, the Lady Hero's gentlewoman, by the name of Hero; she leans me out at her mistress's chamber-window, bids me a thousand times good night,—I tell this tale vilely:—I should first tell thee how the prince, Claudio, and my master, planted and placed and possessed by my master Don John, saw afar off in the orchard this amiable encounter.

Conrade. And thought they Margaret was Hero? 138

Borachio. Two of them did, the prince and Claudio; but the devil my master knew she was Margaret: and partly by his oaths, which first possessed them, partly by the dark night, which did deceive them, but chiefly by my villany, which did confirm any slander that Don John had made, away went Claudio enraged; swore he would meet her, as he was appointed, next morning at the temple, and there, before the whole congregation, shame her with what he saw o'er-night and send her home again without a husband.

1 *Watch.* We charge you, in the prince's name, stand!

2 *Watch.* Call up the right master constable. We have here recovered the most dangerous piece of lechery that ever was known in the commonwealth. 151

1 *Watch.* And one Deformed is one of them: I know him; a' wears a lock.

Conrade. Masters, masters,—

2 *Watch.* You 'll be made bring Deformed forth, I warrant you.

Conrade. Masters,—

1 *Watch.* Never speak; we charge you, let us obey you to go with us.

Borachio. We are like to prove a goodly commodity, being taken up of these men's bills. 161

Conrade. A commodity in question, I warrant you.—Come, we 'll obey you. [*Exeunt.*

Scene IV. *Hero's Apartment.*

Enter HERO, MARGARET, *and* URSULA.

Hero. Good Ursula, wake my cousin Beatrice, and desire her to rise.

Ursula. I will, lady.

Hero. And bid her come hither.

Ursula. Well.   [*Exit.*

Margaret. Troth, I think your other rabato were better.

Hero. No, pray thee, good Meg, I'll wear this.

Margaret. By my troth, 's not so good; and I warrant your cousin will say so.

Hero. My cousin's a fool, and thou art another; I'll wear none but this.

Margaret. I like the new tire within excellently, if the hair were a thought browner; and your gown's a most rare fashion, i' faith. I saw the Duchess of Milan's gown that they praise so.

Hero. O, that exceeds, they say.

Margaret. By my troth, 's but a night-gown in respect of yours: cloth o' gold, and cuts, and laced with silver, set with pearls, down sleeves, side sleeves, and skirts round, underborne with a bluish tinsel; but for a fine, quaint, graceful, and excellent fashion, yours is worth ten on 't.

Hero. God give me joy to wear it! for my heart is exceeding heavy.

Margaret. 'T will be heavier soon by the weight of a man.

Hero. Fie upon thee! art not ashamed?

Margaret. Of what, lady? of speaking honourably? Is not marriage honourable in a beggar? Is not your lord honourable without marriage? I think you would have me say, 'saving your reverence, a husband:' an bad thinking do not wrest true speaking, I'll offend nobody; is there any harm in 'the heavier for a husband?' None, I think,

ACT III. SCENE IV.

an it be the right husband and the right wife; otherwise 't is light, and not heavy: ask my Lady Beatrice else; here she comes.

Enter BEATRICE.

Hero. Good morrow, coz.

Beatrice. Good morrow, sweet Hero.

Hero. Why, how now? do you speak in the sick tune?

Beatrice. I am out of all other tune, methinks.

Margaret. Clap 's into 'Light o' love;' that goes without a burden: do you sing it, and I 'll dance it.

Beatrice. Yea, light o' love, with your heels! then, if your husband have stables enough, you 'll see he shall lack no barns.

Margaret. O illegitimate construction! I scorn that with my heels.

Beatrice. 'T is almost five o'clock, cousin; 't is time you were ready. By my troth, I am exceeding ill; heigh-ho!

Margaret. For a hawk, a horse, or a husband?

Beatrice. For the letter that begins them all, H.

Margaret. Well, an you be not turned Turk, there 's no more sailing by the star.

Beatrice. What means the fool, trow?

Margaret. Nothing I; but God send every one their heart's desire!

Hero. These gloves the count sent me; they are an excellent perfume.

Beatrice. I am stuffed, cousin; I cannot smell.

Margaret. A maid, and stuffed! there 's goodly catching of cold.

Beatrice. O, God help me! God help me! how long have you professed apprehension?

Margaret. Ever since you left it. Doth not my wit become me rarely?

Beatrice. It is not seen enough, you should wear it in your cap. By my troth, I am sick.

Margaret. Get you some of this distilled Carduus Benedictus, and lay it to your heart; it is the only thing for a qualm.

Hero. There thou prickest her with a thistle.

Beatrice. Benedictus! why Benedictus? you have some moral in this Benedictus. 71

Margaret. Moral! no, by my troth, I have no moral meaning; I meant, plain holy-thistle. You may think perchance that I think you are in love; nay, by 'r lady, I am not such a fool to think what I list, nor I list not to think what I can, nor indeed I cannot think, if I would think my heart out of thinking, that you are in love, or that you will be in love, or that you can be in love. Yet Benedick was such another, and now is he become a man; he swore he would never marry, and yet now, in despite of his heart, he eats his meat without grudging: and how you may be converted I know not, but methinks you look with your eyes as other women do.

Beatrice. What pace is this that thy tongue keeps? 83

Margaret. Not a false gallop.

Enter URSULA.

Ursula. Madam, withdraw; the prince, the count, Signior Benedick, Don John, and all the gallants of the town, are come to fetch you to church.

Hero. Help to dress me, good coz, good Meg, good Ursula. [*Exeunt.*

SCENE V. *Another Room in Leonato's House.*
Enter LEONATO, *with* DOGBERRY *and* VERGES.

Leonato. What would you with me, honest neighbour?

Dogberry. Marry, sir, I would have some confidence with you that decerns you nearly.

Leonato. Brief, I pray you; for you see it is a busy time with me.

Dogberry. Marry, this it is, sir.
Verges. Yes, in truth it is, sir.
Leonato. What is it, my good friends?
Dogberry. Goodman Verges, sir, speaks a little off the matter: an old man, sir, and his wits are not so blunt as, God help, I would desire they were; but, in faith, honest as the skin between his brows.
Verges. Yes, I thank God I am as honest as any man living that is an old man and no honester than I.
Dogberry. Comparisons are odorous; palabras, neighbour Verges.
Leonato. Neighbours, you are tedious.
Dogberry. It pleases your worship to say so, but we are the poor duke's officers; but truly, for mine own part, if I were as tedious as a king, I could find it in my heart to bestow it all of your worship.
Leonato. All thy tediousness on me, ah?
Dogberry. Yea, an 't were a thousand pound more than 't is; for I hear as good exclamation on your worship as of any man in the city; and though I be but a poor man, I am glad to hear it.
Verges. And so am I.
Leonato. I would fain know what you have to say.
Verges. Marry, sir, our watch to-night, excepting your worship's presence, ha' ta'en a couple of as arrant knaves as any in Messina.
Dogberry. A good old man, sir; he will be talking: as they say, when the age is in, the wit is out. God help us! it is a world to see.—Well said, i' faith, neighbour Verges: well, God's a good man; an two men ride of a horse, one must ride behind.—An honest soul, i' faith, sir; by my troth he is, as ever broke bread; but God is to be worshipped; all men are not alike; alas, good neighbour!
Leonato. Indeed, neighbour, he comes too short of you.
Dogberry. Gifts that God gives.

Leonato. I must leave you.

Dogberry. One word, sir: our watch, sir, have indeed comprehended two aspicious persons, and we would have them this morning examined before your worship.

Leonato. Take their examination yourself and bring it me: I am now in great haste, as it may appear unto you.

Dogberry. It shall be suffigance.

Leonato. Drink some wine ere you go. Fare you well.

Enter a Messenger.

Messenger. My lord, they stay for you to give your daughter to her husband. 50

Leonato. I'll wait upon them; I am ready.

[*Exeunt Leonato and Messenger.*

Dogberry. Go, good partner, go, get you to Francis Seacole; bid him bring his pen and inkhorn to the gaol: we are now to examine those men.

Verges. And we must do it wisely.

Dogberry. We will spare for no wit, I warrant you: here's that shall drive some of them to a non-come: only get the learned writer to set down our excommunication, and meet me at the gaol. [*Exeunt.*

THE CATHEDRAL OF MESSINA.

ACT IV.

Scene I. *A Church.*

Enter Don Pedro, Don John, Leonato, Friar Francis. Claudio, Benedick, Hero, Beatrice, *and* Attendants.

Leonato. Come, Friar Francis, be brief; only to the plain form of marriage, and you shall recount their particular duties afterwards.

Friar Francis. You come hither, my lord, to marry this lady.

Claudio. No.

Leonato. To be married to her; friar, you come to marry her.

Friar Francis. Lady, you come hither to be married to this count. 10

Hero. I do.

Friar Francis. If either of you know any inward impediment why you should not be conjoined, I charge you, on your souls, to utter it.

Claudio. Know you any, Hero?

Hero. None, my lord.

Friar Francis. Know you any, count?

Leonato. I dare make his answer, none.

Claudio. O, what men dare do! what men may do! what men daily do, not knowing what they do! 20

Benedick. How now! interjections? Why, then, some be of laughing, as, ah, ha, he!

Claudio. Stand thee by, friar.—Father, by your leave:
Will you with free and unconstrained soul
Give me this maid, your daughter?

Leonato. As freely, son, as God did give her me.

Claudio. And what have I to give you back, whose worth
May counterpoise this rich and precious gift?

Don Pedro. Nothing, unless you render her again.

Claudio. Sweet prince, you learn me noble thankfulness.
There, Leonato, take her back again: 31
Give not this rotten orange to your friend;
She's but the sign and semblance of her honour.
Behold how like a maid she blushes here!
O, what authority and show of truth
Can cunning sin cover itself withal!
Comes not that blood as modest evidence
To witness simple virtue? Would you not swear,

All you that see her, that she were a maid,
By these exterior shows? But she is none:
She knows the heat of a luxurious bed;
Her blush is guiltiness, not modesty.
   Leonato. What do you mean, my lord?
   Claudio.   Not to be married,
Not to knit my soul to an approved wanton.
   Leonato. Dear my lord, if you, in your own proof,
Have vanquish'd the resistance of her youth,
And made defeat of her virginity,—
   Claudio. I know what you would say. No, Leonato,
I never tempted her with word too large;
But, as a brother to his sister, show'd
Bashful sincerity and comely love.
   Hero. And seem'd I ever otherwise to you?
   Claudio. Out on thy seeming! I will write against it:
You seem to me as Dian in her orb,
As chaste as is the bud ere it be blown;
But you are more intemperate in your blood
Than Venus, or those pamper'd animals
That rage in savage sensuality.
   Hero. Is my lord well, that he doth speak so wide?
   Leonato. Sweet prince, why speak not you?
   Don Pedro.   What should I speak?
I stand dishonour'd, that have gone about
To link my dear friend to a common stale.
   Leonato. Are these things spoken, or do I but dream?
   Don John. Sir, they are spoken, and these things are true
   Benedick. This looks not like a nuptial.
   Hero.   True! O God!
   Claudio. Leonato, stand I here?
Is this the prince? is this the prince's brother?
Is this face Hero's? are our eyes our own?
   Leonato. All this is so; but what of this, my lord?
   Claudio. Let me but move one question to your daughter;

And, by that fatherly and kindly power
That you have in her, bid her answer truly.
  Leonato. I charge thee do so, as thou art my child.
  Hero. O, God defend me! how am I beset!—
What kind of catechising call you this?
  Claudio. To make you answer truly to your name.
  Hero. Is it not Hero? Who can blot that name
With any just reproach?
  Claudio.   Marry, that can Hero;
Hero itself can blot out Hero's virtue.
What man was he talk'd with you yesternight
Out at your window betwixt twelve and one?
Now, if you are a maid, answer to this.
  Hero. I talk'd with no man at that hour, my lord.
  Don Pedro. Why, then are you no maiden.—Leonato,
I am sorry you must hear: upon mine honour,
Myself, my brother, and this grieved count
Did see her, hear her, at that hour last night
Talk with a ruffian at her chamber-window;
Who hath indeed, most like a liberal villain,
Confess'd the vile encounters they have had
A thousand times in secret.
  Don John. Fie, fie! they are not to be nam'd, my lord,
Not to be spoke of;
There is not chastity enough in language
Without offence to utter them.—Thus, pretty lady,
I am sorry for thy much misgovernment.
  Claudio. O Hero, what a Hero hadst thou been,
If half thy outward graces had been plac'd
About thy thoughts and counsels of thy heart!
But fare thee well, most foul, most fair! farewell,
Thou pure impiety and impious purity!
For thee I'll lock up all the gates of love,
And on my eyelids shall conjecture hang,
To turn all beauty into thoughts of harm,
And never shall it more be gracious.

Leonato. Hath no man's dagger here a point for me?
                                                              [*Hero swoons.*
Beatrice. Why, how now, cousin! wherefore sink you down?
Don John. Come, let us go. These things, come thus to light,
Smother her spirits up.
                        [*Exeunt Don Pedro, Don John, and Claudio.*
Benedick. How doth the lady?
Beatrice.   Dead, I think.—Help, uncle!—
Hero! why, Hero!—Uncle!—Signior Benedick!—Friar!
Leonato. O Fate! take not away thy heavy hand.
Death is the fairest cover for her shame
That may be wish'd for.
Beatrice.   How now, cousin Hero!
Friar Francis. Have comfort, lady.
Leonato. Dost thou look up?
Friar Francis. Yea, wherefore should she not?
Leonato. Wherefore! Why, doth not every earthly thing
Cry shame upon her? Could she here deny
The story that is printed in her blood?—
Do not live, Hero; do not ope thine eyes:
For, did I think thou wouldst not quickly die,
Thought I thy spirits were stronger than thy shames,
Myself would, on the rearward of reproaches,
Strike at thy life. Griev'd I, I had but one?
Chid I for that at frugal nature's frame?
O, one too much by thee! Why had I one?
Why ever wast thou lovely in my eyes?
Why had I not with charitable hand
Took up a beggar's issue at my gates,
Who smirched thus and mir'd with infamy,
I might have said 'No part of it is mine;
This shame derives itself from unknown loins?'
But mine, and mine I lov'd, and mine I prais'd,
And mine that I was proud on, mine so much

That I myself was to myself not mine,
Valuing of her,—why, she, O, she is fallen
Into a pit of ink, that the wide sea
Hath drops too few to wash her clean again,
And salt too little which may season give   140
To her foul-tainted flesh!
    Benedick.   Sir, sir, be patient.
For my part, I am so attir'd in wonder,
I know not what to say.
    Beatrice. O, on my soul, my cousin is belied!
    Benedick. Lady, were you her bedfellow last night?
    Beatrice. No, truly not; although, until last night,
I have this twelvemonth been her bedfellow.
    Leonato. Confirm'd, confirm'd! O, that is stronger made
Which was before barr'd up with ribs of iron!
Would the two princes lie, and Claudio lie,   150
Who lov'd her so, that, speaking of her foulness,
Wash'd it with tears? Hence from her! let her die.
    Friar Francis. Hear me a little;
For I have only silent been so long,
And given way unto this course of fortune,
By noting of the lady: I have mark'd
A thousand blushing apparitions
To start into her face, a thousand innocent shames
In angel whiteness bear away those blushes;
And in her eye there hath appear'd a fire,   160
To burn the errors that these princes hold
Against her maiden truth.—Call me a fool;
Trust not my reading nor my observations,
Which with experimental seal doth warrant
The tenour of my book; trust not my age,
My reverence, calling, nor divinity,
If this sweet lady lie not guiltless here
Under some biting error.
    Leonato.   Friar, it cannot be.

Thou seest that all the grace that she hath left
Is that she will not add to her damnation
A sin of perjury; she not denies it:
Why seek'st thou then to cover with excuse
That which appears in proper nakedness?
   Friar Francis. Lady, what man is he you are accus'd of?
   Hero. They know that do accuse me; I know none:
If I know more of any man alive
Than that which maiden modesty doth warrant,
Let all my sins lack mercy!—O my father,
Prove you that any man with me convers'd
At hours unmeet, or that I yesternight
Maintain'd the change of words with any creature,
Refuse me, hate me, torture me to death!
   Friar Francis. There is some strange misprision in the
      princes.
   Benedick. Two of them have the very bent of honour;
And if their wisdoms be misled in this,
The practice of it lives in John the bastard,
Whose spirits toil in frame of villanies.
   Leonato. I know not. If they speak but truth of her,
These hands shall tear her; if they wrong her honour,
The proudest of them shall well hear of it.
Time hath not yet so dried this blood of mine,
Nor age so eat up my invention,
Nor fortune made such havoc of my means,
Nor my bad life reft me so much of friends,
But they shall find, awak'd in such a kind,
Both strength of limb and policy of mind,
Ability in means and choice of friends,
To quit me of them throughly.
   Friar Francis.   Pause awhile,
And let my counsel sway you in this case.
Your daughter here the princes left for dead:
Let her awhile be secretly kept in,

And publish it that she is dead indeed;
Maintain a mourning ostentation,
And on your family's old monument
Hang mournful epitaphs, and do all rites
That appertain unto a burial.

Leonato. What shall become of this? what will this do?

Friar Francis. Marry, this well carried shall on her behalf
Change slander to remorse; that is some good:
But not for that dream I on this strange course, 210
But on this travail look for greater birth.
She dying, as it must be so maintain'd,
Upon the instant that she was accus'd,
Shall be lamented, pitied, and excus'd
Of every hearer; for it so falls out
That what we have we prize not to the worth
Whiles we enjoy it, but being lack'd and lost,
Why, then we rack the value, then we find
The virtue that possession would not show us
Whiles it was ours. So will it fare with Claudio: 220
When he shall hear she died upon his words,
The idea of her life shall sweetly creep
Into his study of imagination,
And every lovely organ of her life
Shall come apparell'd in more precious habit,
More moving, delicate, and full of life,
Into the eye and prospect of his soul,
Than when she liv'd indeed; then shall he mourn,
If ever love had interest in his liver,
And wish he had not so accused her, 230
No, though he thought his accusation true.
Let this be so, and doubt not but success
Will fashion the event in better shape
Than I can lay it down in likelihood.
But if all aim but this be levell'd false,
The supposition of the lady's death

Will quench the wonder of her infamy;
And if it sort not well, you may conceal her,
As best befits her wounded reputation,
In some reclusive and religious life, 240
Out of all eyes, tongues, minds, and injuries.
  Benedick. Signior Leonato, let the friar advise you;
And though you know my inwardness and love
Is very much unto the prince and Claudio,
Yet, by mine honour, I will deal in this
As secretly and justly as your soul
Should with your body.
  Leonato.   Being that I flow in grief,
The smallest twine may lead me.
  Friar Francis. 'T is well consented: presently away;
For to strange sores strangely they strain the cure.— 250
Come, lady, die to live: this wedding-day
Perhaps is but prolong'd; have patience and endure.
                          [Exeunt all but Benedick and Beatrice.
  Benedick. Lady Beatrice, have you wept all this while?
  Beatrice. Yea, and I will weep a while longer.
  Benedick. I will not desire that.
  Beatrice. You have no reason; I do it freely.
  Benedick. Surely I do believe your fair cousin is wronged.
  Beatrice. Ah, how much might the man deserve of me that would right her!
  Benedick. Is there any way to show such friendship? 260
  Beatrice. A very even way, but no such friend.
  Benedick. May a man do it?
  Beatrice. It is a man's office, but not yours.
  Benedick. I do love nothing in the world so well as you; is not that strange?
  Beatrice. As strange as the thing I know not. It were as possible for me to say I loved nothing so well as you: but believe me not; and yet I lie not; I confess nothing, nor I deny nothing.—I am sorry for my cousin.

Benedick. By my sword, Beatrice, thou lovest me. 270

Beatrice. Do not swear by it, and eat it.

Benedick. I will swear by it that you love me; and I will make him eat it that says I love not you.

Beatrice. Will you not eat your word?

Benedick. With no sauce that can be devised to it. I protest I love thee.

Beatrice. Why, then, God forgive me!

Benedick. What offence, sweet Beatrice?

Beatrice. You have stayed me in a happy hour; I was about to protest I loved you. 280

Benedick. And do it with all thy heart.

Beatrice. I love you with so much of my heart that none is left to protest.

Benedick. Come, bid me do any thing for thee.

Beatrice. Kill Claudio.

Benedick. Ha! not for the wide world.

Beatrice. You kill me to deny it. Farewell.

Benedick. Tarry, sweet Beatrice.

Beatrice. I am gone, though I am here; there is no love in you.—Nay, I pray you, let me go. 290

Benedick. Beatrice,—

Beatrice. In faith, I will go.

Benedick. We'll be friends first.

Beatrice. You dare easier be friends with me than fight with mine enemy.

Benedick. Is Claudio thine enemy?

Beatrice. Is he not approved in the height a villain, that hath slandered, scorned, dishonoured my kinswoman? O that I were a man! What, bear her in hand until they come to take hands; and then, with public accusation, uncovered slander, unmitigated rancour,—O God, that I were a man! I would eat his heart in the market-place. 302

Benedick. Hear me, Beatrice,—

Beatrice. Talk with a man out at a window! A proper saying!

Benedick. Nay, but, Beatrice,—

Beatrice. Sweet Hero! She is wronged, she is slandered, she is undone.

Benedick. Beat—

Beatrice. Princes and counties! Surely, a princely testimony, a goodly count, Count Comfect; a sweet gallant, surely! O that I were a man for his sake! or that I had any friend would be a man for my sake! But manhood is melted into courtesies, valour into compliment, and men are only turned into tongue, and trim ones too; he is now as valiant as Hercules that only tells a lie and swears it.—I cannot be a man with wishing, therefore I will die a woman with grieving.

Benedick. Tarry, good Beatrice. By this hand, I love thee.

Beatrice. Use it for my love some other way than swearing by it.

Benedick. Think you in your soul the Count Claudio hath wronged Hero?

Beatrice. Yea, as sure as I have a thought or a soul.

Benedick. Enough, I am engaged; I will challenge him. I will kiss your hand, and so I leave you. By this hand, Claudio shall render me a dear account. As you hear of me, so think of me. Go, comfort your cousin; I must say she is dead: and so, farewell. [*Exeunt.*

SCENE II. *A Prison.*

Enter DOGBERRY, VERGES, *and* Sexton, *in gowns; and the* Watch, *with* CONRADE *and* BORACHIO.

Dogberry. Is our whole dissembly appeared?

Verges. O, a stool and a cushion for the sexton.

Sexton. Which be the malefactors?

Dogberry. Marry, that am I and my partner.

Verges. Nay, that's certain; we have the exhibition to examine.

Sexton. But which are the offenders that are to be examined? let them come before master constable.

Dogberry. Yea, marry, let them come before me.—What is your name, friend?

Borachio. Borachio.

Dogberry. Pray, write down, Borachio.—Yours, sirrah?

Conrade. I am a gentleman, sir, and my name is Conrade.

Dogberry. Write down, master gentleman Conrade.—Masters, do you serve God?

Conrade. }
Borachio. } Yea, sir, we hope.

Dogberry. Write down, that they hope they serve God: and write God first; for God defend but God should go before such villains!—Masters, it is proved already that you are little better than false knaves; and it will go near to be thought so shortly. How answer you for yourselves?

Conrade. Marry, sir, we say we are none.

Dogberry. A marvellous witty fellow, I assure you; but I will go about with him.—Come you hither, sirrah; a word in your ear: sir, I say to you, it is thought you are false knaves.

Borachio. Sir, I say to you we are none.

Dogberry. Well, stand aside.—Fore God, they are both in a tale.—Have you writ down, that they are none?

Sexton. Master constable, you go not the way to examine: you must call forth the watch that are their accusers.

Dogberry. Yea, marry, that 's the eftest way.—Let the watch come forth.—Masters, I charge you, in the prince's name, accuse these men.

1 Watch. This man said, sir, that Don John, the prince's brother, was a villain.

Dogberry. Write down Prince John a villain. Why, this is flat perjury, to call a prince's brother villain.

Borachio. Master constable,—

Dogberry. Pray thee, fellow, peace; I do not like thy look, I promise thee.

Sexton. What heard you him say else?

2 Watch. Marry, that he had received a thousand ducats of Don John for accusing the Lady Hero wrongfully.

Dogberry. Flat burglary as ever was committed.

Verges. Yea, by the mass, that it is.

Sexton. What else, fellow?

1 Watch. And that Count Claudio did mean, upon his words, to disgrace Hero before the whole assembly, and not marry her. 50

Dogberry. O villain! thou wilt be condemned into everlasting redemption for this.

Sexton. What else?

Watch. This is all.

Sexton. And this is more, masters, than you can deny. Prince John is this morning secretly stolen away; Hero was in this manner accused, in this very manner refused, and upon the grief of this suddenly died.—Master constable, let these men be bound, and brought to Leonato's; I will go before and show him their examination. [*Exit.*

Dogberry. Come, let them be opinioned. 61

Verges. Let them be in the hands—

Conrade. Off, coxcomb!

Dogberry. God's my life, where's the sexton? let him write down the prince's officer coxcomb.—Come, bind them. —Thou naughty varlet!.

Conrade. Away! you are an ass, you are an ass. 67

Dogberry. Dost thou not suspect my place? dost thou not suspect my years?—O that he were here to write me down an ass!—But, masters, remember that I am an ass; though it be not written down, yet forget not that I am an ass.— No, thou villain, thou art full of piety, as shall be proved upon thee by good witness. I am a wise fellow, and, which is more, an officer; and, which is more, a householder; and, which is more, as pretty a piece of flesh as any is in Messina, and one that knows the law, go to; and a rich fellow

94 MUCH ADO ABOUT NOTHING.

enough, go to; and a fellow that hath had losses; and one that hath two gowns and every thing handsome about him. —Bring him away.—O that I had been writ down an ass!

[*Exeunt*

LUDOVICO ARIOSTO (see p. 10).

HERO'S TOMB.

ACT V.

SCENE I. *Before Leonato's House.*

Enter LEONATO *and* ANTONIO.

Antonio. If you go on thus, you will kill yourself;
And 't is not wisdom thus to second grief
Against yourself.

Leonato.   I pray thee, cease thy counsel,
Which falls into mine ears as profitless
As water in a sieve : give not me counsel;
Nor let no comforter delight mine ear
But such a one whose wrongs do suit with mine.
Bring me a father that so lov'd his child,
Whose joy of her is overwhelm'd like mine,
And bid him speak of patience ;
Measure his woe the length and breadth of mine,
And let it answer every strain for strain,
As thus for thus, and such a grief for such,
In every lineament, branch, shape, and form :
If such a one will smile and stroke his beard,
Bid sorrow wag, cry 'hem !' when he should groan,
Patch grief with proverbs, make misfortune drunk
With candle-wasters ; bring him yet to me,
And I of him will gather patience.
But there is no such man : for, brother, men
Can counsel and speak comfort to that grief
Which they themselves not feel ; but, tasting it,
Their counsel turns to passion, which before
Would give preceptial medicine to rage,
Fetter strong madness in a silken thread,
Charm ache with air and agony with words.
No, no ; 't is all men's office to speak patience
To those that wring under the load of sorrow,
But no man's virtue nor sufficiency
To be so moral when he shall endure
The like himself. Therefore give me no counsel ;
My griefs cry louder than advertisement.
  Antonio. Therein do men from children nothing differ.
  Leonato. I pray thee, peace. I will be flesh and blood :
For there was never yet philosopher
That could endure the toothache patiently,
However they have writ the style of gods
And made a push at chance and sufferance

ACT V. SCENE I.

Antonio. Yet bend not all the harm upon yourself;
Make those that do offend you suffer too.
Leonato. There thou speak'st reason; nay, I will do so.
My soul doth tell me Hero is belied,
And that shall Claudio know; so shall the prince
And all of them that thus dishonour her.
Antonio. Here comes the prince and Claudio hastily.

Enter DON PEDRO *and* CLAUDIO.

Don Pedro. Good den, good den.
Claudio. Good day to both of you.
Leonato. Hear you, my lords,—
Don Pedro. We have some haste, Leonato.
Leonato. Some haste, my lord! well, fare you well, my lord:
Are you so hasty now? well, all is one.
Don Pedro. Nay, do not quarrel with us, good old man.
Antonio. If he could right himself with quarrelling,
Some of us would lie low.
Claudio. Who wrongs him?
Leonato. Marry, thou dost wrong me; thou dissembler,
    thou!—
Nay, never lay thy hand upon thy sword;
I fear thee not.
Claudio. Marry, beshrew my hand,
If it should give your age such cause of fear;
In faith, my hand meant nothing to my sword.
Leonato. Tush, tush, man, never fleer and jest at me;
I speak not like a dotard nor a fool,
As under privilege of age to brag
What I have done being young, or what would do
Were I not old. Know, Claudio, to thy head,
Thou hast so wrong'd mine innocent child and me
That I am forc'd to lay my reverence by,
And, with grey hairs and bruise of many days,
Do challenge thee to trial of a man.

G

I say thou hast belied mine innocent child:
Thy slander hath gone through and through her heart,
And she lies buried with her ancestors;
O, in a tomb where never scandal slept, 70
Save this of hers, fram'd by thy villany!

   Claudio. My villany?

   Leonato.   Thine, Claudio; thine, I say.

   Don Pedro. You say not right, old man.

   Leonato.   My lord, my lord,
I 'll prove it on his body, if he dare,
Despite his nice fence and his active practice,
His May of youth and bloom of lustihood.

   Claudio. Away! I will not have to do with you.

   Leonato. Canst thou so daff me? Thou hast kill'd my child;
If thou kill'st me, boy, thou shalt kill a man.

   Antonio. He shall kill two of us, and men indeed: 80
But that 's no matter; let him kill one first;
Win me and wear me; let him answer me.
Come, follow me, boy; come, sir boy, come, follow me:
Sir boy, I 'll whip you from your foining fence;
Nay, as I am a gentleman, I will.

   Leonato. Brother,—

   Antonio. Content yourself. God knows I lov'd my niece;
And she is dead, slander'd to death by villains,
That dare as well answer a man indeed
As I dare take a serpent by the tongue,— 90
Boys, apes, braggarts, Jacks, milksops!

   Leonato.   · Brother Antony,—

   Antonio. Hold you content. What, man! I know them, yea,
And what they weigh, even to the utmost scruple,—
Scambling, out-facing, fashion-monging boys,
That lie and cog and flout, deprave and slander,
Go anticly, show outward hideousness,

ACT V. SCENE I.

And speak off half a dozen dangerous words,
How they might hurt their enemies, if they durst;
And this is all.
  Leonato. But, brother Antony,—
  Antonio. Come, 't is no matter:
Do not you meddle; let me deal in this.
  Don Pedro. Gentlemen both, we will not wake your patience.—
My heart is sorry for your daughter's death;
But, on my honour, she was charg'd with nothing
But what was true and very full of proof.
  Leonato. My lord, my lord,—
  Don Pedro. I will not hear you.
  Leonato. No? Come, brother, away! I will be heard.
  Antonio. And shall, or some of us will smart for it.
      [*Exeunt Leonato and Antonio.*
  Don Pedro. See, see; here comes the man we went to seek.

Enter BENEDICK.

  Claudio. Now, signior, what news?
  Benedick. Good day, my lord.
  Don Pedro. Welcome, signior: you are almost come to part almost a fray.
  Claudio. We had like to have had our two noses snapped off with two old men without teeth.
  Don Pedro. Leonato and his brother. What thinkest thou? Had we fought, I doubt we should have been too young for them.
  Benedick. In a false quarrel there is no true valour. I came to seek you both.
  Claudio. We have been up and down to seek thee; for we are high-proof melancholy, and would fain have it beaten away. Wilt thou use thy wit?
  Benedick. It is in my scabbard; shall I draw it?
  Don Pedro. Dost thou wear thy wit by thy side?

Claudio. Never any did so, though very many have been beside their wit. I will bid thee draw, as we do the minstrels; draw, to pleasure us.

Don Pedro. As I am an honest man, he looks pale.—Art thou sick, or angry?

Claudio. What, courage, man! What though care killed a cat, thou hast mettle enough in thee to kill care.

Benedick. Sir, I shall meet your wit in the career, an you charge it against me. I pray you choose another subject.

Claudio. Nay, then, give him another staff; this last was broke cross.

Don Pedro. By this light, he changes more and more; I think he be angry indeed.

Claudio. If he be, he knows how to turn his girdle.

Benedick. Shall I speak a word in your ear?

Claudio. God bless me from a challenge!

Benedick. [*Aside to Claudio*] You are a villain; I jest not: I will make it good how you dare, with what you dare, and when you dare. Do me right, or I will protest your cowardice. You have killed a sweet lady, and her death shall fall heavy on you. Let me hear from you.

Claudio. Well, I will meet you, so I may have good cheer.

Don Pedro. What, a feast, a feast?

Claudio. I' faith, I thank him: he hath bid me to a calf's head and a capon; the which if I do not carve most curiously, say my knife's naught.—Shall I not find a woodcock too?

Benedick. Sir, your wit ambles well; it goes easily.

Don Pedro. I'll tell thee how Beatrice praised thy wit the other day. I said, thou hadst a fine wit: 'True,' said she, 'a fine little one.' 'No,' said I, 'a great wit:' 'Right,' says she, 'a great gross one.' 'Nay,' said I, 'a good wit:' 'Just,' said she, 'it hurts nobody.' 'Nay,' said I, 'the gentleman is wise:' 'Certain,' said she, 'a wise gentleman.' 'Nay,' said I, 'he hath the tongues:' 'That I believe,' said she, 'for he swore a thing to me on Monday night, which he forswore on Tuesday morning; there 's a double tongue; there 's two tongues.' Thus did she, an hour together, trans-shape thy particular virtues; yet at last she concluded with a sigh, thou wast the properest man in Italy. 165

Claudio. For the which she wept heartily and said she cared not.

Don Pedro. Yea, that she did; but yet, for all that, an if she did not hate him deadly, she would love him dearly: the old man's daughter told us all.

Claudio. All, all; and, moreover, God saw him when he was hid in the garden.

Don Pedro. But when shall we set the savage bull's horns on the sensible Benedick's head?

Claudio. Yea, and text underneath, 'Here dwells Benedick the married man?' 176

Benedick. Fare you well, boy; you know my mind. I will leave you now to your gossip-like humour; you break jests as braggarts do their blades, which, God be thanked, hurt not.—My lord, for your many courtesies I thank you; I must discontinue your company: your brother the bastard is fled from Messina; you have among you killed a sweet and innocent lady. For my Lord Lackbeard there, he and I shall meet; and, till then, peace be with him. [*Exit.*

Don Pedro. He is in earnest. 185

Claudio. In most profound earnest; and, I 'll warrant you, for the love of Beatrice.

Don Pedro. And hath challenged thee.

Claudio. Most sincerely.

Don Pedro. What a pretty thing man is when he goes in his doublet and hose and leaves off his wit! 191

Claudio. He is then a giant to an ape; but then is an ape a doctor to such a man.

Don Pedro. But, soft you, let me be; pluck up, my heart, and be sad. Did he not say, my brother was fled?

Enter DOGBERRY, VERGES, *and the* Watch, *with* CONRADE *and* BORACHIO.

Dogberry. Come you, sir; if justice cannot tame you, she shall ne'er weigh more reasons in her balance: nay, an you be a cursing hypocrite once, you must be looked to.

Don Pedro. How now? two of my brother's men bound! Borachio one!

Claudio. Hearken after their offence, my lord.

Don Pedro. Officers, what offence have these men done?

Dogberry. Marry, sir, they have committed false report; moreover, they have spoken untruths; secondarily, they are slanders; sixth and lastly, they have belied a lady; thirdly, they have verified unjust things; and, to conclude, they are lying knaves.

Don Pedro. First, I ask thee what they have done; thirdly, I ask thee what's their offence; sixth and lastly, why they are committed; and, to conclude, what you lay to their charge.

Claudio. Rightly reasoned, and in his own division; and, by my troth, there's one meaning well suited.

Don Pedro. Who have you offended, masters, that you are thus bound to your answer? this learned constable is too cunning to be understood: what's your offence?

Borachio. Sweet prince, let me go no farther to mine answer; do you hear me, and let this count kill me. I have deceived even your very eyes: what your wisdoms could not discover, these shallow fools have brought to light; who in the night overheard me confessing to this man how Don John your brother incensed me to slander the Lady Hero, how you were brought into the orchard and saw me court Margaret in Hero's garments, how you disgraced her when you should marry her. My villany they have upon record; which I had rather seal with my death than repeat over to my shame. The lady is dead upon mine and my master's false accusation; and, briefly, I desire nothing but the reward of a villain.

Don Pedro. Runs not this speech like iron through your blood?

Claudio. I have drunk poison whiles he utter'd it.

Don Pedro. But did my brother set thee on to this?

Borachio. Yea, and paid me richly for the practice of it.

Don Pedro. He is compos'd and fram'd of treachery;
And fled he is upon this villany.

Claudio. Sweet Hero! now thy image doth appear
In the rare semblance that I lov'd it first.

Dogberry. Come, bring away the plaintiffs; by this time our sexton hath reformed Signior Leonato of the matter; and, masters, do not forget to specify, when time and place shall serve, that I am an ass.

Verges. Here, here comes master Signior Leonato, and the sexton too.

Re-enter LEONATO *and* ANTONIO, *with the* Sexton.

Leonato. Which is the villain? let me see his eyes,
That, when I note another man like him,
I may avoid him; which of these is he?

Borachio. If you would know your wronger, look on me.

Leonato. Art thou the slave that with thy breath hast kill'd
Mine innocent child?

Borachio.   Yea, even I alone.

Leonato. No, not so, villain; thou beliest thyself:
Here stand a pair of honourable men;
A third is fled, that had a hand in it.—
I thank you, princes, for my daughter's death:
Record it with your high and worthy deeds;
'T was bravely done, if you bethink you of it.

Claudio. I know not how to pray your patience;
Yet I must speak. Choose your revenge yourself;
Impose me to what penance your invention

Can lay upon my sin: yet sinn'd I not
But in mistaking.
　　Don Pedro.　　By my soul, nor I;　　　　260
And yet, to satisfy this good old man,
I would bend under any heavy weight
That he 'll enjoin me to.
　　Leonato. I cannot bid you bid my daughter live;
That were impossible: but, I pray you both,
Possess the people in Messina here
How innocent she died; and if your love
Can labour aught in sad invention,
Hang her an epitaph upon her tomb
And sing it to her bones, sing it to-night.—　　270
To-morrow morning come you to my house,
And since you could not be my son-in-law,
Be yet my nephew: my brother hath a daughter,
Almost the copy of my child that 's dead,
And she alone is heir to both of us;
Give her the right you should have given her cousin,
And so dies my revenge.
　　Claudio.　　　　O noble sir,
Your over-kindness doth wring tears from me!
I do embrace your offer; and dispose
For henceforth of poor Claudio.　　　　280
　　Leonato. To-morrow then I will expect your coming;
To-night I take my leave.—This naughty man
Shall face to face be brought to Margaret,
Who I believe was pack'd in all this wrong,
Hir'd to it by your brother.
　　Borachio.　　　　No, by my soul, she was not,
Nor knew not what she did when she spoke to me,
But always hath been just and virtuous
In any thing that I do know by her.　　　　288
　　Dogberry. Moreover, sir, which indeed is not under white
and black, this plaintiff here, the offender, did call me ass: I

beseech you, let it be remembered in his punishment. And
also, the watch heard them talk of one Deformed; they say
he wears a key in his ear and a lock hanging by it, and borrows money in God's name, the which he hath used so long
and never paid that now men grow hard-hearted and will
lend nothing for God's sake : pray you, examine him upon
that point.

Leonato. I thank thee for thy care and honest pains.

Dogberry. Your worship speaks like a most thankful and
reverend youth ; and I praise God for you.   300

Leonato. There 's for thy pains.

Dogberry. God save the foundation !

Leonato. Go, I discharge thee of thy prisoner, and I thank
thee.

Dogberry. I leave an arrant knave with your worship ;
which I beseech your worship to correct yourself, for the
example of others. God keep your worship! I wish your
worship well ; God restore you to health ! I humbly give
you leave to depart : and if a merry meeting may be wished,
God prohibit it !—Come, neighbour.   310

[*Exeunt Dogberry and Verges.*

Leonato. Until to-morrow morning, lords, farewell.

Antonio. Farewell, my lords ; we look for you to-morrow.

Don Pedro. We will not fail.

Claudio.   To-night I 'll mourn with Hero.

Leonato. [*To the Watch*] Bring you these fellows on.—
We 'll talk with Margaret,
How her acquaintance grew with this lewd fellow.

[*Exeunt, severally.*

SCENE II. *Leonato's Orchard.*

Enter BENEDICK *and* MARGARET, *meeting.*

Benedick. Pray thee, sweet Mistress Margaret, deserve
well at my hands by helping me to the speech of Beatrice.

Margaret. Will you then write me a sonnet in praise of my beauty?

Benedick. In so high a style, Margaret, that no man living shall come over it; for, in most comely truth, thou deservest it.

Margaret. To have no man come over me! why, shall I always keep below stairs?

Benedick. Thy wit is as quick as the greyhound's mouth; it catches.

Margaret. And yours as blunt as the fencer's foils, which hit, but hurt not.

Benedick. A most manly wit, Margaret; it will not hurt a woman; and so, I pray thee, call Beatrice: I give thee the bucklers.

Margaret. Give us the swords; we have bucklers of our own.

Benedick. If you use them, Margaret, you must put in the pikes with a vice; and they are dangerous weapons for maids.

Margaret. Well, I will call Beatrice to you, who I think hath legs.

Benedick. And therefore will come. [*Exit Margaret.*
[Sings]   *The god of love,*
            That sits above,
        And knows me, and knows me,
            How pitiful I deserve,—

I mean in singing; but in loving, Leander the good swimmer, Troilus the first employer of panders, and a whole bookful of these quondam carpet-mongers, whose names yet run smoothly in the even road of a blank verse, why, they were never so truly turned over and over as my poor self in love. Marry, I cannot show it in rhyme; I have tried: I can find out no rhyme to 'lady' but 'baby,' an innocent rhyme; for 'scorn,' 'horn,' a hard rhyme; for 'school,' 'fool,' a babbling rhyme; very ominous endings: no, I was not born under a rhyming planet, nor I cannot woo in festival terms.—

ACT V. SCENE II.

Enter BEATRICE.

Sweet Beatrice, wouldst thou come when I called thee?
  Beatrice. Yea, signior, and depart when you bid me.
  Benedick. O, stay but till then!
  Beatrice. 'Then' is spoken; fare you well now: and yet, ere I go, let me go with that I came; which is, with knowing what hath passed between you and Claudio.
  Benedick. Only foul words; and thereupon I will kiss thee.
  Beatrice. Foul words is but foul wind, and foul wind is but foul breath, and foul breath is noisome; therefore I will depart unkissed.
  Benedick. Thou hast frighted the word out of his right sense, so forcible is thy wit. But I must tell thee plainly, Claudio undergoes my challenge; and either I must shortly hear from him, or I will subscribe him a coward. And, I pray thee now, tell me for which of my bad parts didst thou first fall in love with me?
  Beatrice. For them all together; which maintained so politic a state of evil that they will not admit any good part to intermingle with them. But for which of my good parts did you first suffer love for me?
  Benedick. Suffer love! a good epithet! I do suffer love indeed, for I love thee against my will.
  Beatrice. In spite of your heart, I think; alas, poor heart! If you spite it for my sake, I will spite it for yours; for I will never love that which my friend hates.
  Benedick. Thou and I are too wise to woo peaceably.
  Beatrice. It appears not in this confession; there's not one wise man among twenty that will praise himself.
  Benedick. An old, an old instance, Beatrice, that lived in the time of good neighbours. If a man do not erect in this age his own tomb ere he dies, he shall live no longer in monument than the bell rings and the widow weeps.
  Beatrice. And how long is that, think you?

Benedick. Question: why, an hour in clamour and a quarter in rheum; therefore is it most expedient for the wise, if Don Worm, his conscience, find no impediment to the contrary, to be the trumpet of his own virtues, as I am to myself. So much for praising myself, who, I myself will bear witness, is praiseworthy; and now tell me, how doth your cousin?

Beatrice. Very ill.

Benedick. And how do you?

Beatrice. Very ill too. 80

Benedick. Serve God, love me, and mend. There will I leave you too, for here comes one in haste.

Enter URSULA.

Ursula. Madam, you must come to your uncle. Yonder's old coil at home: it is proved my Lady Hero hath been falsely accused, the prince and Claudio mightily abused; and Don John is the author of all, who is fled and gone. Will you come presently?

Beatrice. Will you go hear this news, signior? 88

Benedick. I will live in thy heart, die in thy lap, and be buried in thy eyes; and moreover I will go with thee to thy uncle's. [*Exeunt.*

SCENE III. *A Church.*

Enter DON PEDRO, CLAUDIO, *and three or four with tapers.*

Claudio. Is this the monument of Leonato?

A Lord. It is, my lord.

Claudio. [Reading out of a scroll]
  Done to death by slanderous tongues
    Was the Hero that here lies;
  Death, in guerdon of her wrongs,
    Gives her fame which never dies.
  So the life that died with shame
  Lives in death with glorious fame. 8

Hang thou there upon the tomb,   [*Affixing it.*
Praising her when I am dumb.
Now, music, sound, and sing your solemn hymn.

Song.

Pardon, goddess of the night,
Those that slew thy virgin knight;
For the which, with songs of woe,
Round about her tomb they go.
    Midnight, assist our moan;
    Help us to sigh and groan,
        Heavily, heavily:
    Graves, yawn and yield your dead,
    Till death be uttered,
        Heavily, heavily.

Claudio. Now, unto thy bones good night!
Yearly will I do this rite.
Don Pedro. Good morrow, masters; put your torches out:
The wolves have prey'd; and look, the gentle day,
Before the wheels of Phœbus, round about
Dapples the drowsy east with spots of grey.
Thanks to you all, and leave us; fare you well.
Claudio. Good morrow, masters; each his several way.
Don Pedro. Come, let us hence, and put on other weeds;
And then to Leonato's we will go.
Claudio. And Hymen now with luckier issue speed's
Than this for whom we render'd up this woe!   [*Exeunt.*

SCENE IV. *A Room in Leonato's House.*

Enter LEONATO, ANTONIO, BENEDICK, BEATRICE, MARGARET,
URSULA, FRIAR FRANCIS, *and* HERO.

Friar Francis. Did I not tell you she was innocent?
Leonato. So are the prince and Claudio, who accus'd her
Upon the error that you heard debated;

But Margaret was in some fault for this,
Although against her will, as it appears
In the true course of all the question.
 Antonio. Well, I am glad that all things sort so well.
 Benedick. And so am I, being else by faith enforc'd
To call young Claudio to a reckoning for it.
 Leonato. Well, daughter, and you gentlewomen all,
Withdraw into a chamber by yourselves,
And when I send for you, come hither mask'd.—
          [*Exeunt Ladies.*
The prince and Claudio promis'd by this hour
To visit me.—You know your office, brother:
You must be father to your brother's daughter,
And give her to young Claudio.
 Antonio. Which I will do with confirm'd countenance.
 Benedick. Friar, I must entreat your pains, I think.
 Friar Francis. To do what, signior?
 Benedick. To bind me, or undo me; one of them.—
Signior Leonato, truth it is, good signior,
Your niece regards me with an eye of favour.
 Leonato. That eye my daughter lent her; 't is most true.
 Benedick. And I do with an eye of love requite her.
 Leonato. The sight whereof I think you had from me,
From Claudio, and the prince; but what 's your will?
 Benedick. Your answer, sir, is enigmatical;
But, for my will, my will is your good will
May stand with ours, this day to be conjoin'd
In the state of honourable marriage,—
In which, good friar, I shall desire your help.
 Leonato. My heart is with your liking.
 Friar Francis.   And my help.—
Here comes the prince and Claudio.

  Enter Don Pedro *and* Claudio, *and two or three others.*
 Don Pedro. Good morrow to this fair assembly.

Leonato. Good morrow, prince; good morrow, Claudio:
We here attend you. Are you yet determin'd
To-day to marry with my brother's daughter?
Claudio. I'll hold my mind, were she an Ethiope.
Leonato. Call her forth, brother; here's the friar ready.
[*Exit Antonio.*
Don Pedro. Good morrow, Benedick. Why, what's the
  matter, 40
That you have such a February face,
So full of frost, of storm, and cloudiness?
Claudio. I think he thinks upon the savage bull.—
Tush, fear not, man; we'll tip thy horns with gold,
And all Europa shall rejoice at thee,
As once Europa did at lusty Jove
When he would play the noble beast in love.
Benedick. Bull Jove, sir, had an amiable low;
And some such strange bull leap'd your father's cow,
And got a calf in that same noble feat 50
Much like to you, for you have just his bleat.
Claudio. For this I owe you; here comes other reckon-
  ings.—

Re-enter ANTONIO, *with the* Ladies *masked.*

Which is the lady I must seize upon?
Antonio. This same is she, and I do give you her.
Claudio. Why, then she's mine.—Sweet, let me see your
  face.
Leonato. No, that you shall not, till you take her hand
Before this friar and swear to marry her.
Claudio. Give me your hand; before this holy friar,
I am your husband, if you like of me.
Hero. And when I liv'd I was your other wife; 60
      [*Unmasking.*
And when you lov'd you were my other husband.
Claudio. Another Hero!

Hero. Nothing certainer;
One Hero died defil'd, but I do live,
And, surely as I live, I am a maid.
　Don Pedro. The former Hero! Hero that is dead!
　Leonato. She died, my lord, but whiles her slander liv'd.
　Friar Francis. All this amazement can I qualify;
When after that the holy rites are ended,
I'll tell you largely of fair Hero's death.
Meantime let wonder seem familiar,
And to the chapel let us presently.
　Benedick. Soft and fair, friar.—Which is Beatrice?
　Beatrice. [*Unmasking*] I answer to that name. What is your will?
　Benedick. Do not you love me?
　Beatrice. Why, no; no more than reason.
　Benedick. Why, then your uncle and the prince and Claudio
Have been deceiv'd; they swore you did.
　Beatrice. Do not you love me?
　Benedick. Troth, no; no more than reason.
　Beatrice. Why, then my cousin, Margaret, and Ursula
Are much deceiv'd; for they did swear you did.
　Benedick. They swore that you were almost sick for me.
　Beatrice. They swore that you were well-nigh dead for me.
　Benedick. 'T is no such matter.—Then you do not love me?
　Beatrice. No, truly, but in friendly recompense.
　Leonato. Come, cousin, I am sure you love the gentleman.
　Claudio. And I'll be sworn upon 't that he loves her;
For here 's a paper written in his hand,
A halting sonnet of his own pure brain,
Fashion'd to Beatrice.

Hero. And here's another,
Writ in my cousin's hand, stolen from her pocket,
Containing her affection unto Benedick.

Benedick. A miracle! here's our own hands against our hearts.—Come, I will have thee; but, by this light, I take thee for pity.

Beatrice. I would not deny you; but, by this good day, I yield upon great persuasion; and partly to save your life, for I was told you were in a consumption.

Benedick. Peace! I will stop your mouth. [*Kissing her.*

Don Pedro. How dost thou, Benedick, the married man?

Benedick. I'll tell thee what, prince; a college of wit-crackers cannot flout me out of my humour. Dost thou think I care for a satire or an epigram? No; if a man will be beaten with brains, he shall wear nothing handsome about him. In brief, since I do purpose to marry, I will think nothing to any purpose that the world can say against it; and therefore never flout at me for what I have said against it; for man is a giddy thing, and this is my conclusion.— For thy part, Claudio, I did think to have beaten thee; but in that thou art like to be my kinsman, live unbruised and love my cousin.

Claudio. I had well hoped thou wouldst have denied Beatrice, that I might have cudgelled thee out of thy single life, to make thee a double-dealer; which, out of question, thou wilt be, if my cousin do not look exceeding narrowly to thee.

Benedick. Come, come, we are friends; let's have a dance ere we are married, that we may lighten our own hearts and our wives' heels.

Leonato. We'll have dancing afterward.

Benedick. First, of my word; therefore play, music.— Prince, thou art sad; get thee a wife, get thee a wife: there is no staff more reverend than one tipped with horn.

Enter a Messenger.

Messenger. My lord, your brother John is ta'en in flight, And brought with armed men back to Messina. 124

Benedick. Think not on him till to-morrow; I'll devise thee brave punishments for him.—Strike up, pipers. [*Dance.*
[*Exeunt.*

ARIOSTO'S INKSTAND.

NOTES.

ABBREVIATIONS USED IN THE NOTES.

Abbott (or Gr.), Abbott's *Shakespearian Grammar* (third edition).
A. S., Anglo-Saxon.
A. V., Authorized Version of the Bible (1611).
B. and F., Beaumont and Fletcher.
B. J., Ben Jonson.
Camb. ed., "Cambridge edition" of *Shakespeare*, edited by Clark and Wright.
Cf. (*confer*), compare.
Coll., Collier (second edition).
Coll. MS., Manuscript Corrections of Second Folio, edited by Collier.
D., Dyce (second edition).
H., Hudson (first edition).
Id. (*idem*, the same.
J. H., John Hunter's edition of *Much Ado About Nothing* (London, 1872).
K., Knight (second edition).
Nares, *Glossary*, edited by Halliwell and Wright (London, 1859).
Prol., Prologue.
S., Shakespeare.
Schmidt, A. Schmidt's *Shakespeare-Lexicon* (Berlin, 1874).
Sr., Singer.
St., Staunton.
Theo., Theobald.
V., Verplanck.
W., White.
Walker, Wm. Sidney Walker's *Critical Examination of the Text of Shakespeare* (London, 1860).
Warb., Warburton.
Wb., Webster's Dictionary (revised quarto edition of 1864).
Worc., Worcester's Dictionary (quarto edition).

The abbreviations of the names of Shakespeare's Plays will be readily understood; as *T. N.* for *Twelfth Night*, *Cor.* for *Coriolanus*, *3 Hen. VI.* for *The Third Part of King Henry the Sixth*, etc. *P. P.* refers to *The Passionate Pilgrim*; *V. and A.* to *Venus and Adonis*; *L. C.* to *Lover's Complaint*; and *Sonn.* to the *Sonnets*.

When the abbreviation of the name of a play is followed by a reference to *page*, Rolfe's edition of the play is meant.

The numbers of the lines (except for *Much Ado*) are those of the "Globe" ed. or Crowell's reprint of that ed.

NOTES.

ACT I.

SCENE I.—The stage-direction in the folio, as in the quarto, reads " *Enter Leonato Gouernour of Messina, Innogen his wife,*" etc.; but as Innogen neither speaks nor is mentioned during the play, Theo. dropped her name from the list of *dramatis personæ*. As he suggests, the poet may at first have intended to introduce her, but afterwards decided to leave her out.

1. *Don Pedro.* Both the quarto and the folio have "Don Peter" here and in 9 below, but elsewhere "Don Pedro."

3. *By this.* Cf. *Macb.* iii. 1. 26: "'Twixt this and supper;" *Lear,* i. 1. 118: "from this for ever," etc.

7. *Sort.* Possibly = rank (Schmidt), as in 29 below. Cf. *Hen. V.* iv. 7. 142, iv. 8. So, etc.

8. *Achiever.* Used by S. nowhere else.

16. *Will be.* For the omission of the relative, see Gr. 244.

Very much glad. We should not now use this expression, though we say "very much pleased," "very much delighted," etc.

19. *Joy could not*, etc. "Of all the transports of joy, that which is attended with tears is least offensive; because, carrying with it this mark of pain, it allays the envy that usually attends another's happiness. This he finely calls a *modest* joy, such an one as did not insult the observer by an indication of happiness unmixed with pain" (Warb.). Capell says that the *joy* "wore the modestest garb that joy can do, that is, silence and tears."

20. *Badge.* Steevens compares Chapman, *Odyssey*, x. :

"our eyes wore
The same wet badge of weak humanity;"

and *Macb.* i. 4. 33 :

"My plenteous joys,
Wanton in fulness, seek to hide themselves
In drops of sorrow."

23. *Kind.* Natural (Schmidt). Cf. *R. of L.* 1423: "Conceit deceitful, so compact, so kind." *Kindness* = tenderness. Cf. *T. N.* ii. 1. 41 : "my bosom is full of kindness, and I am yet so near the manners of my mother that upon the least occasion more mine eyes will tell tales of me."

26. *Montanto.* A term in fencing, meaning, according to Cotgrave, "an upright blow or thrust." Cf. *M. W.* ii. 3. 27 : "thy punto, thy stock, thy reverse, thy distance, thy montant." Steevens cites B. J., *Every Man in his Humour:* "your punto, your reverso, your stoccata, your imbrocata, your passada, your montanto," etc.

29. *Sort.* See on 7 above.

30. *What.* Who; as often, "but only in the predicate" (Schmidt). Cf. *Temp.* v. 1. 185: "What is this maid?" See also *Ham.* p. 253 and cf. Gr. 254.

32. *Pleasant.* Facetious. Cf. *Hen. V.* i. 2. 259: "We are glad the Dauphin is so pleasant with us" (see also 281); *M. for M.* iii. 2. 120: "You are pleasant, sir," etc.

34. *Set up his bills.* That is, posted his challenge, like a prize-fighter. Steevens quotes B. J., *Every Man out of his Humour:* "I have set up my bills without discovery;" and Nash, *Have With You*, etc. : "setting up bills, like a bearward or fencer, what fights we shall have, and what weapons she will meet me at." He also gives this extract from an old MS. : "Item a challenge playde before the King's majestie [Edward VI.] at Westminster, by three maisters, Willyam Pascall, Robert Greene, and W. Browne, at seven kynde of weapons. That is to say, the axe, the pike, the rapier and target, the rapier and cloke, and with two swords, agaynst all alyens and strangers being borne without the King's dominions, of what countrie so ever he or they were, geving them warninge by theyr bills set up by the three maisters, the space of eight weeks before the sayd challenge was playde; and it was holden four severall Sun-

ACT I. SCENE I.

dayes one after another." It appears from the same work that all challenges "to any maister within the realme of Englande being an Englishe man" were against the rules of the "Noble Science of Defence." Saint Paul's was a place where these bills or advertisements were much posted. Nash, in his *Pierce Pennilesse*, speaks of "maisterlesse men that set up theyr bills in Paules for services, and such as paste up theyr papers on every post for arithmetique and writing schooles."

35. *Flight*. That is, shooting with the *flight*, a kind of long and light-feathered arrow used for great distances. S. uses the word in this sense only here, but it is common in writers of the time. Cf. B. and F., *Bonduca*: "not a flight drawn home;" Middleton, *Game of Chess*: "discharg'd it like a flight," etc.

37. *Bird-bolt*. A short, thick, blunt-headed arrow, shot from a cross-bow and used to kill rooks with. Cf. Marston, *What You Will*:

"ignorance should shoot
His gross-knobb'd bird-bolt."

Douce says: "The meaning of the whole is—Benedick, from a vain conceit of his influence over women, challenged Cupid at *roving* (a particular kind of archery in which *flight*-arrows are used); in other words, he challenged him to *shoot at hearts*. The fool, to ridicule this piece of vanity, in his turn challenged Benedick to shoot at crows with the cross-bow and bird-bolt; an inferior kind of archery used by fools, who, for obvious reasons, were not permitted to shoot with pointed arrows: whence the proverb, 'A fool's bolt is soon shot.'" Cf. *A. Y. L.* v. 4. 67 and *Hen. V.* iii. 7. 132. See also *L. L. L.* iv. 3. 25 and *T. N.* i. 5. 100.

39. *To eat*, etc. Cf. *Hen. V.* ii. 7. 99:

"*Rambures*. He longs to eat the English.
Constable. I think he will eat all he kills."

40. *Tax*. Reproach, inveigh against. Cf. *A. Y. L.* ii. 7. 71, 86, *Ham.* i. 4. 18, iii. 3. 29, etc.

41. *Meet with you*. Even with you, a match for you. Steevens says that the expression is common in the midland counties, and quotes Holiday, Τεχνογαμια, 1618: "Go meet her, or else she'll be meet with me."

43. *Victual*. Elsewhere S. uses the plural. Bacon has both "Victual" and "Victuals" in *Essay* xxxiii. Cf. *Exod.* xii. 39 and *Josh.* i. 11.

Holp. S. uses both *helped* and *holp* as past tense and as participle. For the former use of *holp*, see *K. John*, i. 1. 240, *Cor.* v. 3. 63, etc.; and for the latter, *Temp.* i. 2. 63, *Rich. II.* v. 5. 62, *Macb.* i. 6. 23, etc. We find *holpen* in *Ps.* lxxxiii. 8, *Dan.* xi. 34, etc.

44. *Trencher-man*. Cf. *trencher-friend* (= parasite) in *T. of A.* iii. 6. 106, and *trencher-knight* (= waiter) in *L. L. L.* v. 2. 464 (cf. 476); also Lodge, *Wit's Miserie*, 1596: "His doublet is of cast satten cut sometime upon taffata, but that the bumbast hath eaten through it, and spotted here and there with pure fat to testifie that he is a good trencher-man."

49. *Stuffed*. Fully endowed. Cf. *K. and J.* iii. 5. 183: "Stuff'd, as they say, with honourable parts;" and *W. T.* ii. 1. 185: "of stuff'd sufficiency." Edwards observes that Mede, in his *Discourses on Scripture*, speaks of Adam as "he whom God had stuffed with so many excellent qualities." Beatrice uses the word contemptuously = stuffed out, padded.

Farmer says that *a stuffed man* was "one of the many cant phrases for a cuckold."

52. *Stuffing.* Halliwell says: "Beatrice seems to use the term *stuffing* in a sense analogous to the Latin *vestis fartum*; or, possibly, in reference to his mental qualities."

We are all mortal. One of the affected phrases of the time. Cf. *Sir Gyles Goosecappe, Knight*, 1606: "Sir Gyles Goosecap has always a deathes head (as it were) in his mouth, for his onely one reason for every thing is, because wee are all mortall."

57. *Five wits.* The *wits*, or intellectual powers, seem to have been reckoned as five to correspond with the five senses, which were also called *wits*. Cf. Chaucer, *Persones Tale:* "the five wittis; as sight, hereing, smelling, savouring, and touching." Boswell quotes a prayer by Sir Thomas More, in which he asks to be forgiven for his sins "in mispending of my five wittes." Schmidt says that "the proverbial five wits" were "common wit, imagination, fantasy, estimation, memory." In *Sonn.* 141. 9 we find the two meanings distinguished:

> "But my five wits nor my five senses can
> Dissuade one foolish heart from serving thee."

59. *To keep himself warm.* "To have wit enough to keep one's self warm" was a common proverb. Cf. *T. of S.* ii. 1. 268:

> "*Petruchio.* Am I not wise?
> *Katharina.* Yes; keep you warm."

Steevens quotes among other examples of the phrase, B. J., *Cynthia's Revels:* "your whole self cannot but be perfectly wise; for your hands have wit enough to keep themselves warm."

Bear it for a difference. That is, for a mark of distinction; a term in heraldry. Cf. *Ham.* iv. 5. 183: "you must wear your rue with a difference."

62. *Sworn brother.* See *Rich. II.* p. 208 or *A. Y. L.* p. 199.

64. *Faith.* That is, his fidelity as a friend.

65. *Block.* Still the technical term for the wooden model on which hats are shaped. Cf. *Lear*, iv. 6. 187: "this' a good block." See also *Epigrammes by I. D.*, 1596:

> "He weares a hat now of the flat-crowne blocke,
> The treble ruffes, long cloake, and doublet French;
> He takes tobacco, and doth weare a locke;
> And wastes more time in dressing then a wench;"

and Dekker, *Seven Deadly Sinnes of London*, 1606: "the blocke for his head alters faster then the feltmaker can fitte him, and thereupon we are called in scorne blockheads."

66. *Not in your books.* Evidently = not in favour with you, but the origin of the phrase has been much disputed. Johnson gives it "to be in one's codicils or will, to be among friends set down for legacies." Steevens takes the *books* to be memorandum-books, or, perhaps, heraldic records (cf. *T. of S.* ii. 1. 225). Farmer says "*to be in a man's books* originally meant to be in the list of his *retainers.*" K. explains it as a commercial allusion—one to whom you give credit. Schmidt, like Steevens,

decides on "books of memory" (1 *Hen. VI.* ii. 4. 101 and 2 *Hen. VI.* i. 1. 100), which seems the most plausible explanation.

68. *Squarer.* Quarreller, bully. Cf. *square* = quarrel in *M. N. D.* ii. 1. 30, *A. and C.* ii. 1. 45, iii. 3. 41, etc.

74. *Presently.* Immediately; the usual meaning in S. Cf. *Temp.* i. 2. 125, iv. 1. 42, v. 1. 101, etc.

75. *A thousand pound.* See *Rich. II.* p. 182.

77. *Hold friends with you.* Cf. *M. for M.* i. 2. 185:

"Implore her in my voice, that she make friends
To the strict deputy."

89. *Charge.* Burden, incumbrance (Johnson). Douce thinks it means "the person committed to your care."

94. *You have it full.* Schmidt explains this as = "you are the man, you will do," and compares *T. of S.* i. 1. 203; but it seems rather = you get as good as you sent, you are well answered.

95. *Fathers herself.* Is like her father; a phrase common in Dorsetshire (Steevens). For the verb, cf. *J. C.* ii. 1. 297, *Macb.* iv. 2. 27, etc.

101. *Still.* Continually; as in 117 below. Gr. 69.

105. *Is it possible,* etc. Steevens compares *Cor.* ii. 1. 93: "Our very priests must become mockers, if they encounter such ridiculous subjects as you are."

107. *Convert.* For the intransitive use, cf. *R. of L.* 592, *Macb.* iv. 3. 229, *Rich. II.* v. 1. 66, v. 3. 64, etc.

109. *Of.* By. Cf. *Macb.* iii. 6. 27, etc. Gr. 170.

112. *A dear happiness.* True good luck. Cf. *R. and J.* iii. 3. 28: "This is dear mercy."

118. *Scape.* Not "'scape," as often printed. See *Macb.* p. 214 or Wb. s. v.

Predestinate is used by S. nowhere else. For the form, see Gr. 342.

121. *Were.* The Coll. MS. omits the word.

128. *A jade's trick.* Cf. *A. W.* iv. 5. 64: "If I put any tricks upon 'em, sir, they shall be jade's tricks;" *T. and C.* ii. 1. 21: "a red murrain o' thy jade's tricks!" For *jade* = a worthless or vicious horse, see *V. and A.* 391, *J. C.* iv. 2. 26, etc.

139. *I am not of many words.* Cf. *M. for M.* ii. 1. 204: "Are you of fourscore pounds a year?" *Oth.* v. 1. 65: "Are you of good or evil?" Sir J. Hawkins says: "The poet has judiciously marked the gloominess of Don John's character by making him averse to the common forms of civility."

141. *Please it your grace,* etc. Will it please your grace, etc. Cf. *Temp.* iii. 3. 42: "Will 't please you taste of what is here?" The *to* is sometimes inserted; as in iii. 5. 18 below: "It pleases your worship to say so," etc. See Gr. 349.

149. *Tyrant.* That is, one who shows no mercy. Cf. *M. for M.* ii. 4. 169: "I'll prove a tyrant to him."

162. *Sad.* Serious. Cf. *A. Y. L.* iii. 2. 227: "Speak sad brow and true maid." See also i. 3. 54 and ii. 1. 307 below.

Flouting Jack. Cf. *Temp.* iv. 1. 198: "Monster, your fairy, which you say is a harmless fairy, has done little better than played the Jack with us." We have *flouting-stock* (= laughing-stock) in *M. W.* iii. 1. 120 and iv. 5. 83. Cf. the use of *flout* in ii. 3. 132, v. 1. 95, and v. 4. 100 below.

To tell us Cupid is a good hare-finder, etc. This puzzled Johnson and Steevens, but Tollet explains it: "Do you scoff and mock in telling us that Cupid, who is blind, is a good hare-finder, which requires a quick eye-sight; and that Vulcan, a blacksmith, is a rare carpenter?" Schmidt suspects a double meaning in *hare-finder*.

164. *To go in.* To join you in.

168. *No such matter.* Nothing of the kind. See on ii. 3. 198 below.

169. *There's her cousin*, etc. A hint of the half-liking for Beatrice which is hidden under Benedick's depreciation of her.

176. *With suspicion.* That is, "on account of the horns hidden under it" (Schmidt). Cf. 212 and 232 below.

179. *Sigh away Sundays.* "A proverbial expression to signify that a man has no rest at all" (Warb.); or more probably, as Steevens explains it, an allusion to the Puritanic observance of Sunday.

187. *With who?* Cf. "To who?" in *Oth.* i. 2. 52, *Cymb.* iv. 2. 75, etc. Gr. 274.

189. *If this were so*, etc. "If this were the truth, so it would be uttered" (J. H.).

190. *Like the old tale*, etc. Mr. Blakeway gives this *old tale* as he heard it in childhood from his great aunt: "Once upon a time, there was a young lady (called Lady Mary in the story), who had two brothers. One summer they all three went to a country-seat of theirs, which they had not before visited. Among the other gentry in the neighbourhood, who came to see them, was a Mr. Fox, a bachelor, with whom they, particularly the young lady, were much pleased. He used often to dine with them, and frequently invited Lady Mary to come and see his house. One day that her brothers were absent elsewhere, and she had nothing better to do, she determined to go thither, and accordingly set out unattended. When she arrived at the house and knocked at the door, no one answered. At length she opened it, and went in. Over the portal of the hall was written, 'Be bold, be bold, but not too bold.' She advanced—over the staircase, the same inscription. She went up—over the entrance of a gallery, the same. She proceeded—over the door of a chamber, 'Be bold, be bold, but not too bold, lest that your heart's blood should run cold.' She opened it—it was full of skeletons, tubs full of blood, etc. She retreated in haste. Coming down stairs, she saw, out of a window, Mr. Fox advancing towards the house, with a drawn sword in one hand, while with the other he dragged along a young lady by her hair. Lady Mary had just time to slip down and hide herself, under the stairs, before Mr. Fox and his victim arrived at the foot of them. As he pulled the young lady up stairs, she caught hold of one of the bannisters with her hand, on which was a rich bracelet. Mr. Fox cut it off with his sword: the hand and bracelet fell into Lady Mary's lap, who then contrived to escape unobserved, and got home safe to her brothers' house.

"After a few days Mr. Fox came to dine with them, as usual (whether by invitation, or of his own accord, this deponent saith not). After

ACT I. SCENE I.

dinner, when the guests began to amuse each other with extraordinary anecdotes, Lady Mary at length said she would relate to them a remarkable dream she had lately had. 'I dreamed,' said she, 'that as you, Mr. Fox, had often invited me to your house, I would go there one morning. When I came to the house, I knocked, etc., but no one answered. When I opened the door, over the hall was written, "Be bold, be bold, but not too bold." But,' said she, turning to Mr. Fox, and smiling, 'it is not so, nor it was not so.' Then she pursues the rest of the story, concluding at every turn with, 'It is not so, nor it was not so,' till she comes to the room full of dead bodies, when Mr. Fox took up the burden of the tale, and said, 'It is not so, nor it was not so, and God forbid it should be so;' which he continues to repeat at every subsequent turn of the dreadful story, till she comes to the circumstance of his cutting off the young lady's hand; when, upon his saying, as usual, 'It is not so, nor it was not so, and God forbid it should be so,' Lady Mary retorts, 'But it is so, and it was so, and here the hand I have to show,' at the same time producing the hand and bracelet from her lap: whereupon, the guests drew their swords, and instantly cut Mr. Fox into a thousand pieces."

195. *To fetch me in.* Schmidt explains this "to take me in, to dupe me;" that is, to entrap me into a confession.

198. *Spoke.* The quarto reading; the folio has "speake." As Steevens remarks, Benedick means that he spoke his mind when he said "God forbid it should be so!"

208. *In the force of his will.* "Warburton's professional eye first detected the allusion here to heresy, as defined in scholastic divinity; according to which it was not merely heterodox opinion, but a wilful adherence to such opinion. The subject was a familiar one in Shakespeare's day" (W.). For a different but less probable explanation, see Schmidt.

212. *Recheat.* Notes sounded on the horn to call off the hounds. *Winded*=blown. The meaning is, I will not wear a horn on my forehead which the huntsman may blow (Johnson).

213. *Baldrick.* A *baldrick* was a belt, girdle, or sash, sometimes a sword-belt; generally passed round one side of the neck and under the opposite arm. Turbervile, in his *Book of Hunting*, ed. 1611, gives a figure of a huntsman with his horn hanging from a baldrick worn in that way. Sylvester (*Du Bartas*) calls the zodiac "heaven's baldrick." Cf. Spenser, *Prothalamion:*

"That like the twins of Jove, they seem'd in sight,
Which decke the Bauldricke of the Heavens bright."

The *invisibility* of the horns of the cuckold is often alluded to by the old writers, as Halliwell shows by many quotations.

215. *Fine.* End, conclusion. For the play on the word, cf. *Ham.* v. 1. 115: "the fine of his fines."

222. *A ballad-maker's pen.* Referred to contemptuously as a worthless instrument (Halliwell).

225. *Argument.* Subject (that is, for satire). Cf. *M. N. D.* iii. 2. 242:

"If you have any pity, grace, or manners,
You would not make me such an argument;"

and 1 *Hen. IV.* ii. 2. 100: "it would be argument for a week, laughter for a month, and a good jest for ever."

226. *Like a cat.* Shooting at a cat hung up in a bottle or a basket was one of the "manly sports" of the olden time. Steevens quotes *Warres, or the Peace is Broken:* "arrowes flew faster than they did at a catte in a basket;" and *Cornu-copiæ*, 1623: "bowmen bold, which at a cat do shoot."

228. *Adam.* Alluding to Adam Bell, an outlaw whose fame as an archer is celebrated in a ballad which may be found in Percy's *Reliques*.

230. *In time,* etc. The line is taken from *The Spanish Tragedy*, where it reads, "In time the savage bull sustains the yoke." It had appeared even earlier in Watson's *Passionate Centurie of Love*, 1582. In the original copy (*MS. Harl.* 3277) it reads, "In tyme the bull is brought to beare the yoake," but it was afterwards printed "weare the yoake." Cf. Ovid, *Tristia*, iv. 6. 1: "Tempore ruricolae patiens fit taurus aratri;" and *De Arte Amandi*, i. 471: "Tempore difficiles veniunt ad aratra juvenci."

240. *In Venice.* Venice was then "the capital of pleasure and intrigue," as Paris is now. Cf. Greene, *Never Too Late:* "this great city of Venice is holden Loves Paradice."

242. *You will temporize*, etc. You will come to terms in the course of time. Cf. *T. and C.* iv. 4. 6: "If I could temporize with my affection," etc.

248. *Tuition.* Guardianship; the etymological meaning. S. uses the word nowhere else.

252. *Guarded.* Faced, bordered. *Guards* were trimmings or facings of lace or embroidery. Cf. *M. of V.* ii. 2. 164:

"Give him a livery
More guarded than his fellows':"

Hen. VIII. prol. 16: "In a long motley coat guarded with yellow;" *L. L. L.* iv. 3. 58: "O, rhymes are guards on wanton Cupid's hose," etc.

253. *Flout old ends.* Make sport of old endings of letters, like those just quoted by Claudio and Don Pedro. Reed cites Barnaby Googe's dedication to the first edition of *Palingenius*, 1560: "And thus committing your Ladiship with all yours to the tuicion of the most mercifull God, I ende. From Staple Inne at London, the eighte and twenty of March." Malone adds Drayton's ending of a letter to Drummond of Hawthornden, in 1619: "And so wishing you all happiness, I commend you to God's tuition, and rest your assured friend." Cf. *R. of L.* 1308, where Lucrece ends her letter thus:

"So I commend me from our house in grief;
My woes are tedious, though my words are brief."

Examine your conscience. "Examine if your sarcasms do not touch yourself" (Johnson).

257. *Thine to teach.* "Ready to be taught by you" (J. H.). Walker conjectured "use" for *teach*, but no change is called for.

262. *Affect.* Love. Cf. *T. G. of V.* iii. 1. 82:

"There is a lady in Verona here
Whom I affect." etc.

263. *Went onward.* Started.

267. *And that.* For the use of *that*, see Gr. 285.

271. *To wars,*— We adopt the pointing of Coll., Halliwell, and W. Don Pedro interrupts Claudio in his fine-twisted story.

275. *Break with her.* Broach the subject to her. Cf. *T. G. of V.* i. 3. 44: "now will we break with him;" *Hen. VIII.* v. 1. 47: "Have broken with the king," etc. S. uses *break to* in the same sense; as in 292 just below. He also has *break with* = break one's word to; as in *M. W.* iv. 3. 2. 57: "we have appointed to dine with Mistress Anne, and I would not break with her for more money than I'll speak of."

The words *and with her father, And thou shalt have her*, omitted in the folio, were restored by Theo.

281. *Salv'd.* Palliated. Cf. *Cor.* iii. 2. 70:

"you may salve so,
Not what is dangerous present, but the loss
Of what is past."

Treatise. Discourse, talk. Cf. *V. and A.* 774: "Your treatise makes me like you worse and worse;" *Macb.* v. 5. 12: "a dismal treatise" (that is, tale).

283. *The fairest grant,* etc. "The best boon is that which answers the necessities of the case" (St.); or *what will serve is fit*, as the next line gives it. Hayley suggested "to necessity." Hanmer reads "plea," and the Coll. MS. "ground" for *grant*.

284. *'T is once.* "Once for all; 't is enough to say at once" (Steevens); or "'t is a fact past all help" (Schmidt). So in *C. of E.* iii. 1. 89, "Once this" = this much is certain.

287. *I will assume thy part,* etc. Where is this spoken? In the next scene Antonio tells Leonato that a servant of his had overheard the conversation in an alley in his orchard; and in the *next* scene Borachio tells John that *he* had overheard it from behind an arras in the house. Are we to suppose an interval of time between the first and second scenes of this act? Or were there two conversations between the Prince and Claudio on this subject? Or is it one of those instances of the poet's carelessness in the minor parts of his plot to which reference has already been made in *M. N. D.* p. 122 and *Ham.* p. 241?

289. *Unclasp my heart.* Cf. *T. N.* i. 4. 13:

"I have unclasp'd
To thee the book even of my secret soul."

See also *W. T.* iii. 2. 168.

290. *Take her hearing prisoner,* etc. Cf. *Cymb.* i. 6. 103: "Takes prisoner the wild motion of mine eye."

292. *After.* Afterwards. Cf. *Temp.* ii. 2. 10: "And after bite me," etc. Gr. 26.

294. *Presently.* See on 74 above.

SCENE II.—4. *Strange.* The quarto reading; omitted in the folio.

5. *They.* S. uses *news* both as singular and as plural. Cf. *Temp.* v. 1. 221, *Rich. II.* iii. 4. 74, 82, *Cor.* i. 1. 4, etc., with *Hen. VIII.* ii. 2. 39, *Oth.* ii. 2. 7, etc. See also ii. 1. 155 below: "these ill news;" and v. 2. 88: "this news."

8. *Thick-pleached.* Thickly interwoven. Cf. iii. 1. 7 below: "the pleached bower;" *A. and C.* iv. 14. 73: "with pleach'd arms" (that is, folded arms).

Orchard. Garden; the only meaning Schmidt recognizes in S. See *J. C.* p. 142.

9. *Thus much overheard.* The quarto reading; the folio has "thus overheard."

10. *Discovered.* Revealed. Cf. *Lear,* ii. 1. 68: "I threaten'd to discover him," etc.

13. *By the top.* Cf. *A. W.* v. 3. 39: "Let 's take the instant by the forward top."

For *break with,* see on i. 1. 275 above.

17. *Till it appear itself.* Till it appear as a reality. H. suggests "approve" for *appear.*

18. *Withal.* With it. Cf. *T. G. of V.* ii. 7. 67: "he will scarce be pleas'd withal," etc. Gr. 196.

21. *Cousins.* "Cousins were anciently enrolled among the dependants, if not domestics, of great families, such as that of Leonato. Petruchio, while intent on the subjection of Katharine [*T. of S.* iv. 1. 154] calls out, in terms imperative, for his 'cousin Ferdinand'" (Steevens). For the use of *cousin* in S. see *Ham.* p. 179 or *A. Y. L.* p. 147.

Cry you mercy. Beg your pardon. See *M. N. D.* p. 159.

SCENE III.—1. *The good year.* Supposed to be corrupted from *goujère* and = "Pox on 't!" (*T. A.* iii. 4. 308). Cf. *M. W.* i. 4. 129, *Lear,* v. 3. 24, etc. The expression was, however, often used literally; as in Holyband's *French Littleton,* ed. 1609: "God give you a good morrow and a good yeare,—*Dieu vous doit bon jour et bon an.*" Halliwell adds several similar examples.

4. *Breeds it.* The *it* is not found in the early eds. but is given in the Coll. MS.

8. *At least.* The quarto reading; the folio has "yet."

11. *Born under Saturn.* An astrological allusion. Those born under Saturn were supposed to be of a phlegmatic or *saturnine* disposition. Cf. *T. A.* ii. 3. 31:

"though Venus govern your desires,
Saturn is dominator over mine."

See also 2 *Hen. IV.* ii. 4. 286.

Goest about. Dost undertake. See *M. N. D.* p. 177 or *Hen. V.* p. 174.

12. *Mortifying.* Used in the literal sense = killing. Cf. *M. of V.* i. 1. 82: "mortifying groans." See also *Hen. V.* i. 1. 26.

I cannot hide, etc. "This is one of our author's natural touches. An envious and unsocial mind, too proud to give pleasure and too sullen to receive it, always endeavours to hide its malignity from the world and from itself under the plainness of simple honesty or the dignity of haughty independence" (Johnson).

14. *Stomach.* Appetite; as in ii. 3. 232 below. See also *T. G. of V.* i. 2. 68, *T. of S.* iv. 1. 161, etc.

16. *Claw.* Tickle, flatter. The origin of the metaphor is illustrated

ACT I. SCENE III.

by 2 *Hen. IV.* ii. 4. 282. See also *L. L. L.* iv. 2. 66. Reed quotes Wilson, *Discourse upon Usury*, 1572 : "therefore I will clawe him, and saye well might he fare, and godds blessing have he too. For the more he speaketh, the better it itcheth, and maketh better for me."

18. *Controlment.* Constraint. Cf. *T. A.* ii. 1. 68 and *K. John*, i. 1. 20.

20. *Grace.* Favour; as in ii. 3. 26 below: "one woman shall not come in my grace," etc.

23. *Canker.* Canker-rose, or dog-rose. It is similarly contrasted with the cultivated rose in *Sonn.* 54. 5 :

"The canker-blooms have full as deep a dye
As the perfumed tincture of the roses ;"

and in 1 *Hen. IV.* i. 3. 176 :

"To put down Richard, that sweet lovely rose,
And plant this thorn, this canker, Bolingbroke?"

24. *Blood.* Disposition, temper. Cf. 2 *Hen. IV.* iv. 4. 38: "When you perceive his blood inclin'd to mirth," etc.

25. *Carriage.* Bearing, deportment. Cf. *C. of E.* iii. 2. 14: "Teach sin the carriage of a holy saint," etc.

Rob love from any. Cf. *Sonn.* 35. 14: "that sweet thief which sourly robs from me ;" and *Rich. II.* i. 3. 173 : "Which robs my tongue from breathing native breath."

34. *For I use it only.* "For I make nothing else my counsellor" (Steevens). For *I make* the folio has "I will make."

40. *Model.* Cf. 2 *Hen. IV.* i. 3. 42 :

"When we mean to build,
We first survey the plot, then draw the model ;
And when we see the figure of the house,
Then must we rate the cost of the erection ;
Which if we find outweighs ability,
What do we then but draw anew the model," etc.

41. *What is he for a fool?* What sort of fool is he? St. quotes B. J., *Every Man out of his Humour*, iii. 6 : "What is he for a creature?" and *Ram Alley*, iv. 2 : "What is he for a man?"

43. *Marry.* See *M. of V.* p. 138.

46. *Proper.* For the ironical use, cf. iv. 1. 304 below : "a proper saying !" See also *Hen. VIII.* i. 1. 98, *Macb.* iii. 4. 60, etc. And for the contemptuous *squire*, cf. 1 *Hen. VI.* iv. 1. 23, *Oth.* iv. 2. 145, etc.

50. *March-chick.* That is, a chicken hatched in March ; a sneer at his *forwardness*.

52. *Entertained for.* Employed as. Cf. *T. of A.* iv. 3. 496 : "To entertain me as your steward still ;" *Lear*, iii. 6. 83 : "You, sir, I entertain for one of my hundred," etc.

Smoking a musty room is suggestive of the uncleanly habits of the time. Steevens quotes Burton, *Anat. of Melancholy :* "the smooke of juniper is in great request with us at Oxford, to sweeten our chambers." In a letter from the Lords of the Council in the reign of Edward VI. we are told that Lord Paget's house was so small that "after one month it would wax unsavory for hym to contynue in ;" and in the correspondence of the Earl of Shrewsbury with Lord Burleigh, during the confinement of Mary Queen of Scots at Sheffield Castle, in 1572, we learn that she was to be removed for five or six days "to klense her chambar, being kept very unklenly." Again, in a memoir written by Anne Countess of Dorset, in 1603, we read: "we all went to Tibbals to see the Kinge, who used my mother and my aunt very gratiouslie; but we all saw a great chaunge betweene the fashion of the Court as it was now, and of y^t in ye Queene's, for we were all lowzy by sittinge in Sr Thomas Erskin's chamber."

53. *Me.* For the "ethical dative," see Gr. 220.

54. *Sad.* Serious, earnest. See on i. 1. 162 above.

Arras. Tapestry hangings, so called from Arras in France. Cf. *Ham.* ii. 2. 163, iii. 3. 28, etc.

59. *Start-up.* Used by S. nowhere else. *Upstart* occurs as a noun in 1 *Hen. VI.* iv. 7. 87, and as an adjective in *Rich. II.* ii. 3. 122.

"In the character of the chief villain of the drama, the Poet has wholly departed from the plot of Bandello's tale, which furnished him with the outline of the story. The novelist had ascribed the base deception, on which his story turns, to the revenge of a rejected lover, who, at the catastrophe, makes some amends for his guilt, by remorse and frank confession. Shakespeare has chosen to pourtray a less common and obvious, but unhappily too true character,—one of sullen malignity, to whom the happiness or success of others is sufficient reason for the bitterness of hatred, and cause enough to prompt to injury and crime. This character has much the appearance of being the original conception and rough sketch of that wayward, dark disposition, which the Poet afterwards painted more elaborately, with some variation of circumstances and temperament, in his 'honest Iago'" (V.).

61. *Sure.* To be relied on. Cf. *Cor.* i. 1. 176:

"you are no surer, no,
Than is the coal of fire upon the ice,
Or hailstone in the sun."

63. *Cheer.* Festive enjoyment. For the original meaning of the word, see *M. of V.* p. 152 or *M. N. D.* p. 163.

65. *Go prove.* See *A. Y. L.* p. 137, note on *Go buy.*

ACT II.

SCENE I.—4. *Heart-burned.* "The pain commonly called the *heartburn* proceeds from an *acid* humour in the stomach, and is therefore properly enough imputed to *tart* looks" (Johnson). Cf. Falstaff's jesting use of the word in 1 *Hen. IV.* iii. 3. 59.

17. *Shrewd.* Shrewish. Cf. *J. C.* p. 145. *Curst* has the same meaning, and the two words are used interchangeably and in combination. In the *T. of S.* the heroine is called "Katharine the curst" (i. 2. 128) or "Kate the curst" (ii. 1. 87), and "curst and shrewd" (i. 1. 185, i. 2. 70). See also *M. N. D.* p. 167.

ACT II. SCENE I.

24. *Just.* Just so, exactly so. Cf. *A. Y. L.* iii. 2. 281 : "Yes, just." See also *M. for M.* iii. 1. 68, *Hen. V.* iii. 7. 158, etc.

27. *In the woollen.* That is, between the blankets, without sheets.

35. *Bear-herd.* The early eds. have "Berrord," which probably indicates the common pronunciation. The Coll. MS. gives "bear-ward," which some prefer. Schmidt says that *bear-herd* is "the Shakespearian form of the word." The folio has "Beare-heard" in *T. of S.* ind. ii. 21 and 2 *Hen. IV.* i. 2. 192. In 2 *Hen. VI.* v. 1. 149 it has "Berard," and in 210 "Bearard." These are the only passages in which the word occurs. For *bearward*, see quotation in note on i. 1. 34 above.

The *apes* rode on the bear led about by the *bear-herd.* For the idea that old maids led apes into hell, cf. *T. of S.* ii. 1. 34.

41. *For the heavens.* Some take this to be an oath, as in *M. of V.* ii. 2. 12 : "for the heavens, rouse up a brave mind."

45. *Curtsy.* The same word as *courtesy*, which some eds. give here. The quarto has "cursie" in both instances in this speech, and Halliwell prints "cursey," which he says is "a genuine archaic form of the word *courtesy*." See also on iv. 1. 314 below.

48. *Father.* Omitted in the folio.

52. *To be overmastered with.* To have as master, to be ruled by. For *with* = by, see Gr. 193.

53. *To make an account.* To render an account. The folio omits *an.*

54. *I'll none.* Cf. *M. N. D.* iii. 2. 169: "keep thy Hermia; I will none;" *A. and C.* ii. 5. 9: "I'll none now," etc. For other ellipses with *will*, see Gr. 405.

56. *Match.* Marry. Cf. *T. N.* i. 3. 116: "she'll none o' the count; she'll not match above her degree," etc.

60. *Important.* Importunate. Cf. *C. of E.* v. 1. 138: "your important letters;" *A. W.* iii. 7. 21 : "his important blood." In *Lear*, iv. 4. 26, the quartos have "important," the folio "importun'd."

61. *Measure.* Moderation, a proper limit; with a play on the other meaning of a dance, as in *L. L. L.* iv. 3. 384 and *Rich. II.* iii. 4. 7.

63. *Cinque-pace.* A kind of dance, as the context shows. Cf. *T. N.* i. 3. 139 and see *Ham.* p. 222. The Camb. ed. quotes Marston, *Insatiate Countess*, ii. :

> "Thinke of me as of the man
> Whose dancing dayes you see are not yet done.
> *Len.* Yet, you sinke a pace, sir."

For *sink* in 68 below the Coll. MS. has "sink apace." According to Nares, the *cinque-pace* was the same as the *galliard*. See *Hen. V.* p. 150.

65. *Mannerly.* Also used adverbially in *M. of V.* ii. 9. 100 and *Cymb.* iii. 6. 92.

66. *Ancientry.* "The port and behaviour of old age" (Schmidt). "It means old people in *W. T.* iii. 3. 63 : "wronging the ancientry."

75. *So.* Provided that. Gr. 133.

81. *Favour.* Face, look ; as in iii. 3. 17 below. Cf. *M. for M.* iv. 2. 34 : "for surely, sir, a good favour you have, but that you have a hanging look," etc.

Defend. Forbid, like the Fr. *défendre*. Cf. iv. 2. 18 below. See also

I

Oth. i. 3. 267: "And heaven defend your good souls, that you think," etc.

83. *Philemon's roof.* An allusion to the story of Philemon and Baucis in Ovid. Cf. *A. Y. L.* iii. 3. 10: "worse than Jove in a thatched house." This and the next two speeches form a rhymed couplet in the fourteen-syllable measure of Golding's translation of Ovid. For *Jove* the folio misprints "Love."

86. *Well, I would,* etc. This speech, with the next two here assigned to Balthazar, is given to *Benedick* in the early eds. Theo. made the correction.

89. *Which is one?* We should now say "*What* is one?"

96. *Clerk.* The reader of responses in the English church service; suggested here by Balthazar's "Amen." Cf. *Sonn.* 85. 6: "And like unlettered clerk still cry 'Amen;'" *Rich. II.* iv. 1. 173: "Am I both priest and clerk? Well then, Amen."

100. *At a word.* Cf. *M. W.* i. 1. 109: "at a word, he hath, believe me;" *Cor.* i. 3. 122: "No, at a word, madam," etc.

103. *Do him so ill-well.* That is, mimic his bad manner so well. Steevens compares *M. of V.* i. 2. 63: "a better bad habit of frowning."

104. *Dry hand.* Formerly regarded as the mark of a cold nature. Cf. *T. N.* i. 3. 77.

Up and down. Thoroughly, exactly. Cf. *T. G. of V.* ii. 3. 32: "here's my mother's breath up and down;" *T. of S.* iv. 3. 89: "What, up and down, carv'd like an apple-tart?" *T. A.* v. 2. 107: "For up and down she doth resemble thee."

109. *There's an end.* There is no more to be said about it. Cf. *Hen. V.* ii. 1. 11, iii. 2. 153, etc. *There an end* is used in the same sense; as in *T. of S.* v. 2. 98, *Rich. II.* v. 1. 69, etc.

112. *Nor will you not.* For the double negative, see Gr. 406.

115. *The Hundred Merry Tales.* A popular jest-book of the time, an imperfect copy of which was discovered and reprinted in 1815.

117. *What's he?* Who's he? See on i. 1. 30 above.

123. *Only his gift is.* His talent is only. For the transposition, cf. *J. C.* v. 4. 12: "Only I yield to die," etc. Gr. 420.

Impossible slanders are "such as, from their absurdity and impossibility, bring their own confutation with them" (Johnson). Warb. wished to read "impassable" = "so ill invented that they will pass upon nobody."

125. *He both pleases,* etc. "By his impious jests, she insinuates, he *pleased* libertines; and by his *devising slanders* of them, he angered them" (Warb.).

127. *In the fleet.* J. H. explains this as "connected with this" (see 114-116 above); but it simply means in the company, and the figure is carried out in *boarded* = accosted. Cf. *Ham.* ii. 2. 170: "I'll board him presently," etc.

132. *Partridge wing.* Formerly considered the most delicate part of the bird (Halliwell). Some eds. print "partridge' wing."

145. *Near.* Intimate with. Cf. *Rich. III.* iii. 4. 14: "you and he are

near in love;" 2 *Hen. IV.* v. 1. 81: "I would humour his men with the imputation of being near their master," etc.

146. *Enamoured.* Followed by *on* also in 1 *Hen. IV.* v. 2. 70 and 2 *Hen. IV.* i. 3. 102; by *of* in *M. N. D.* iii. 1. 141, iv. 1. 82, and *K. and J.* iii. 3. 2. Cf. Gr. 181.

155. *News.* For the number, see on i. 2. 5 above.

159. *Use.* Third person imperative; or "subjunctive used optatively or imperatively," as Abbott (Gr. 364, 365) calls it.

162. *Faith melteth into blood.* Fidelity is melted in the heat of passion. For *blood* in this sense, cf. ii. 3. 150 and iv. 1. 56 below. See also *A. Y. L.* v. 4. 59, *A. W.* iii. 7. 21, etc.

163. *Proof.* Experience. Cf. *J. C.* ii. 1. 21: "'t is a common proof;" *Ham.* iv. 7. 113: "passages of proof," etc.

169. *Willow.* For other allusions to the willow as the emblem of unhappy love, see *M. of V.* v. 1. 10, 3 *Hen. VI.* iii. 3. 228, iv. 1. 100, *Oth.* iv. 3. 28 fol., v. 2. 248, etc. Cf. Spenser, *F. Q.* i. 1. 9: "The Willow worne of forlorne Paramours;" Lyly, *Sappho and Phao*, ii. 4: "Enjoy thy care in covert; weare willow in thy hat, and bayes in thy heart;" Swan, *Speculum Mundi*, 1635: "it is yet a custom that he which is deprived of his love must wear a willow garland." Fuller, in his *Worthies*, describes the willow as "a sad tree, whereof such who have lost their love, make their mourning garlands, and we know what exiles hung up their harps upon such dolefull supporters. The twiggs hereof are physick to drive out the folly of children," etc.

170. *County.* Count; the reading of the quarto here and in 317 below. The folio has "Count" here, and "Counte" there, but "Counties" in iv. 1. 310. *County* is also found in *M. of V.* i. 2. 49, *A. W.* iii. 7. 22, *T. N.* i. 5. 320, and often in *R. and J.* Cf. Warner, *Albions England* "Horne and Egmond, counties brave."

171. *An usurer's chain.* Gold chains were often worn by wealthy citizens in the poet's time, as they are now on public occasions by the aldermen of London (Reed).

175. *Drovier.* The spelling of both quarto and folio.

187. *Though bitter.* The reading of the early eds., changed by Johnson to "the bitter."

Puts the world, etc. Assumes to represent the world, and thus reports me. For *gives me out*, cf. *A. W.* ii. 3. 16: "That gave him out incurable," etc.

193. *A lodge in a warren.* The hut occupied by a watchman in a rabbit warren. Steevens remarks: "A parallel thought occurs in the first chapter of *Isaiah*, where the prophet, describing the desolation of Judah, says, 'The daughter of Zion is left as a cottage in a vineyard, as a lodge in a garden of cucumbers.' I am informed that near Aleppo these lonely buildings are still made use of, it being necessary that the fields where water-melons, cucumbers, etc., are raised should be regularly watched. I learn from Tho. Newton's *Herball to the Bible*, 1587, that 'so soone as the cucumbers, etc., be gathered, these lodges are abandoned of the watchmen and keepers, and no more frequented.' From these forsaken buildings, it should seem, the prophet takes his comparison."

213. *Hath a quarrel to you.* Cf. *T. N.* iii. 4. 248 : " I am sure no man hath any quarrel to me ;" *Cor.* iv. 5. 133 : " Had we no quarrel else to Rome," etc.

216. *Misused.* Abused, reviled. Cf. *A. Y. L.* iv. 1. 205 : " you have simply misused our sex," etc.

218. *My very visor,* etc. Steevens notes a similar thought in Statius, *Thebaid,* v. 658 :

"ipsa insanire videtur
Sphynx galeae custos."

221. *Impossible conveyance.* " Incredible dexterity" (St.). Warb. would read "impassable," as in 123 above ; Hanmer, "impetuous ; " Johnson "importable" (=insupportable), a word used by Spenser (*F. Q.* ii. 8. 35 : "importable powre") and other writers of the time. No change is necessary. The meaning, as Malone remarks, is " with a rapidity equal to that of *jugglers,* who appear to perform *impossibilities.*" *Conveyance* was often used in the sense of sleight of hand, trickery. Cf. 3 *Hen. VI.* iii. 3. 160 : " thy sly conveyance," etc.

223. *She speaks poniards.* Cf. *Ham.* iii. 2. 414 : " I will speak daggers to her."

224. *Terminations.* Terms, words ; used by S. only here.

227. *Left.* The Coll. MS. gives "lent."

228. *Have made Hercules have turned.* Cf. *Ham.* v. 1. 268 : " I hop'd thou shouldst have been my Hamlet's wife," etc. Gr. 360.

230. *Ate.* Cf. *K. John,* ii. 1. 63 : " An Ate, stirring him to blood and strife ;" *J. C.* iii. 1. 271 : " With Ate by his side, come hot from hell," etc.

231. *Some scholar,* etc. Because Latin, the language of the church, was used in exorcisms. See *Ham.* p. 172, note on *Scholar.*

232. *A man may live as quiet,* etc. That is, to live in hell would be as quiet as to live in a sanctuary, compared with living where she is, and people sin on purpose in order to escape her in that way.

240. *Toothpicker.* S. also uses *toothpick ;* as in *A. W.* i. 1. 171, *K. John,* i. 1. 190, etc.

241. *Prester John's foot.* Prester or Presbyter John was a mythical Christian king of India. Some placed his dominions in Abyssinia ; Sir John Mandeville locates them in an island called Pentexoire. The difficulty of getting access to him is referred to in *Hudibras :*

" While like the mighty Prester John,
Whose person none dares look upon,
But is preserv'd in close disguise
From being made cheap to vulgar eyes."

The great Cham was the Khan of Tartary. He is associated with Prester John in the old drama of *Fortunatus :*

" And then I 'll revel it with Prester John,
Or banquet with great Cham of Tartary."

Steevens quotes Cartwright, *The Siege,* 1651 : "bid me take the Parthian king by the beard ; or draw an eye-tooth from the jaw royal of the Persian monarch." Cf. the old romance of *Huon of Bourdeaux :* " Thou must goe to the citie of Babylon to the Admiral Gaudisse, to bring me

ACT II. SCENE I. 133

thy hand full of the heare of his beard, and foure of his greatest teeth. Alas, my lord, (quoth the Barrons,) we see well you desire greatly his death, when you charge him with such a message."

242. *The Pigmies.* A race of dwarfs fabled to dwell beyond Mount Imaus in India. Their wars with the cranes are celebrated in a poem ascribed to Homer. Cf. Milton, *P. L.* i. 575:

> "that small infantry
> Warr'd on by cranes;"

and *Id.* i. 780:

> "like that Pygmean race
> Beyond the Indian mount."

251. *Use.* Interest, "usance" (*M. of V.* i. 3. 46, 109, 142). Cf. *V. and A.* 768: "But gold that's put to use more gold begets;" *Sonn.* 134. 10: "Thou usurer, that put'st forth all to use," etc.

263. *Civil count.* Some eds. print "civil, count." The meaning of *civil* is the same in either case, and is perhaps best illustrated by Cotgrave's definition of *aigre-douce* as a "civile orange, or orange that is betweene sweet and sower." Cf. Nash, *Four Letters Confuted*, 1592: "For the order of my life, it is as civil as an orange." There is an obvious play upon *civil* and *Seville*. J. H. explains *civil* as "plain," and compares the use of the word as applied to dress. See *T. N.* iii. 4. 5 and *R. and J.* iii. 2. 10. But the word is not there = "plain, homely," as he makes it, but rather = grave, sober; that is, like civilian dress as distinguished from military dress with its brighter colours and showy trappings.

264. *Jealous complexion.* Cf. the use of *yellowness* = jealousy, in *M. W.* i. 3. 111.

265. *Blazon.* "Explanation" (Schmidt). Cf. *Ham.* i. 5. 21: "this eternal blazon" (this unfolding of the mysteries of eternity).

266. *Conceit.* Conception, idea. Cf. *M. of V.* iii. 4. 2:

> "You have a noble and a true conceit
> Of godlike amity," etc.

273. *Cue.* See *Ham.* p. 213.

281. *Poor fool.* "Formerly an expression of tenderness" (Malone). Cf. *T. G. of V.* iv. 4. 98, *T. N.* v. 1. 377, 3 *Hen. VI.* ii. 5. 36, etc.

285. *Good Lord, for alliance!* This seems to mean "Heaven send me a husband!" (said sportively, of course), as St. explains it; or "Good Lord, how many alliances are forming!" as Boswell gives it.

To go to the world meant to marry; perhaps originally in distinction from going into the church, where celibacy was the rule. Cf. *A. W.* i. 3. 20: "if I may have your ladyship's good will to go to the world," etc. So *a woman of the world* = a married woman, in *A. Y. L.* v. 3. 5.

286. *Sunburnt.* Apparently = "homely, ill-favoured," as St. explains it. Cf. *T. and C.* i. 3. 282:

> "The Grecian dames are sunburnt and not worth
> The splinter of a lance."

287. *Heigh-ho for a husband!* The title of an old ballad, preserved in the Pepysian Collection, Magdalene College, Cambridge (Malone). Cf. iii. 4. 48 below.

296. *Matter.* Sense. Cf. *A. Y. L.* ii. 1. 68: "For then he 's full of matter;" *Ham.* ii. 2. 95: "More matter with less art;" *Lear,* iv. 6. 178: "O matter and impertinency mix'd!"

306. *The melancholy element.* We have many allusions in S. to the old notion that all things were composed of the four elements, earth, air, fire, and water. See *J. C.* p. 185 and *Hen. V.* p. 169. Cf. also *Sonn.* 44. 13, 45. 5, *A. and C.* v. 2. 292, etc.

307. *Sad.* Serious. See on i. 1. 162 above.

309. *Unhappiness.* Theo. changed this to "an happiness;" but Warb. reminds him that the word sometimes meant "a wild, wanton, unlucky trick," and quotes B. and F., *The Maid of the Mill:*

"My dreams are like my thoughts, honest and innocent;
Yours are unhappy."

Schmidt explains *unhappiness* here as "wanton or mischievous tricks," and compares *unhappy* in *A. W.* iv. 5. 66: "A shrewd knave and an unhappy" (that is, "roguish, full of tricks"). Seymour explains the passage thus: "She hath often dreamed of unhappiness, which yet was so short-lived that presently she was merry again and waked herself with laughing."

311. *Hear tell.* "This form of speech, which S. constantly puts into the mouth of personages of the highest rank, but which is now never heard in Old England, except perhaps in the remotest rural districts, is in common use in New England" (W.).

317. *County.* The quarto has "Countie," the folio "Counte." See on i. 1. 170 above.

To go to church. Cf. *M. of V.* iii. 2. 305: "First go with me to church and call me wife," etc.

322. *A just seven-night.* An exact week. Cf. *M. of V.* iv. 1. 327: "a just pound."

324. *Breathing.* Interval, delay. Cf. *R. of L.* 1720: "Untimely breathings."

328. *Mountain of affection.* Johnson was sorely troubled by this colloquial expression, and suggested "mooting." Steevens and Malone think that S. may have written it, as he has "many phrases equally harsh." The discussion fills almost a page of the Var. ed. of 1821.

340. *Strain.* Family, lineage. Cf. *Hen. V.* ii. 4. 51: "he is bred out of that bloody strain;" *J. C.* v. 1. 59: "the noblest of thy strain," etc. See also Spenser, *F. Q.* iv. 8. 33: "Sprung of the aunciencent stocke of Princes straine;" *Id.* v. 9. 32: "yborne of heavenly strene;" *Id.* vi. 6. 9: "bred of hellish strene."

Approved. Proved, tried. Cf. iv. 1. 44 below: "an approved wanton;" also 297: "approved in the height a villain," etc.

344. *Queasy.* Squeamish, fastidious. Cf. *A. and C.* iii. 6. 20: "queasy with his insolence" (that is, sick of it); *Lear,* ii. 1. 19: "of queasy question" (= nice question).

SCENE II.—1. *Shall marry.* Is to marry. Cf. *A. Y. L.* ii. 4. 88, *J. C.* i. 3. 87, etc. Gr. 315.

5. *Medicinable.* Medicinal. Cf. *T. and C.* i. 3. 91: "Sol... whose medicinable eye;" *Oth.* v. 2. 351: "medicinable gum" ("medicinal" in quartos), etc. Gr. 3.

Displeasure to him. Cf. "a quarrel to you" in ii. 1. 213 above. See also Gr. 186. We find "displeasure at" in *Per.* i. 3. 21, and "displeasure against" in *Temp.* iv. 1. 202, *A. Y. L.* i. 2. 90, and *A. W.* iv. 5. 80.

6. *Affection.* Inclination, wish. Whatever thwarts his wishes agrees with mine.

19. *Temper.* Compound, mix. Cf. *R. and J.* iii. 5. 98:

"Madam, if you could find out but a man
To bear a poison, I would temper it;"

Ham. v. 2. 339: "It is a poison temper'd by himself;" *Cymb.* v. 5. 250: "To temper poisons for her."

22. *Estimation.* Worth, merit; as in *A. W.* v. 3. 4, etc. It is used in a concrete sense (=thing of worth) in *T. and C.* ii. 2. 91 and *Cymb.* i. 4. 99.

23. *Stale.* Wanton, harlot; as in iv. 1. 62 below. For another meaning, see *Temp.* p. 137.

25. *Misuse.* Deceive. Cf. *abuse* in v. 2. 85 below: "the prince and Claudio mightily abused." *Abuse* is often used by S. in this sense, *misuse* only in the present passage.

32. *Intend.* Pretend. Cf. *R. of L.* 121: "Intending weariness with heavy spright." See also *T. of S.* iv. 1. 206, *Rich. III.* iii. 5. 8, and *T. of A.* ii. 2. 219. On the other hand, *pretend* was sometimes = intend; as in *R. of L.* 576, *T. G. of V.* ii. 6. 37, etc.

37. *Trial.* That is, verifying it by their own observation. *Instances* =proofs; as in *M. for M.* iv. 3. 134, *T. and C.* v. 2. 153, etc.

39. *Term me Claudio.* Theo. changed *Claudio* to "Borachio," but this does not seem necessary. As Malone remarks, Claudio might suppose that his rival was addressed as Claudio in consequence of a secret agreement between the guilty pair, in order to prevent suspicion if Hero should be overheard.

45. *Grow this.* Let this grow. See Gr. 361.

46. *The working this.* We should now say either "working this" or "the working of this." See Gr. 373.

50. *Presently.* See on i. 1. 74 above; and for *go learn*, on i. 3. 65.

SCENE III.—4. *Orchard.* Garden. See on i. 2. 8 above.

10. *Argument.* Subject. See on i. 1. 225 above.

14. *Ten mile.* Cf. *Macb.* v. 5. 37: "within this three mile;" and see on i. 1. 75 above.

16. *Doublet.* See *A. Y. L.* p. 158.

18. *Orthography.* The abstract for the concrete. Cf. *L. L. L.* i. 2. 190: "I am sure I shall turn sonnet." Pope changed it to "orthographer," and some read "orthographist."

19. *May.* Can. See Gr. 309, and cf. 307.

26. *In my grace.* Into my favour. For *in*, see Gr. 159; and for *grace*, on i. 3. 24 above.

27. *I'll none.* I'll have nothing to do with her. See on ii. 1. 54 above.

28. *Cheapen.* Chaffer for, bid for. Cf. *Per.* iv. 6. 10. "cheapen a kiss of her." In the Shropshire dialect *cheapen*=ask the price of. Cf. Heywood, *Edward IV.:* "I see you come to cheap, and not to buy." Palsgrave gives, "I cheape, I demaunde the price of a thyng that I wolde bye."

29. *Noble . . . angel.* With a punning reference to the two coins, the *noble* and the *angel*. See *Rich. II.* p. 219, note on *Thanks, noble peer*. For the *angel*, see *M. of V.* p. 144.

30. *Her hair,* etc. That is, her hair shall be of the natural colour, not dyed according to the fashion of the time. Stubbes, in his *Anatomie of Abuses,* 1595, says: "If any have haire of her owne naturall growing, which is not faire ynough, then will they die it in divers colours." Or the allusion may be to the wearing of false hair. Cf. iii. 4. 12: "I like the new tire within excellently, if the hair were a thought browner." For the poet's antipathy to false hair, see *M. of V.* p. 149.

32. The quarto has here "*Enter prince, Leonato, Claudio, Musicke,*" and six lines below "*Enter Balthaser with musicke.*" The folio has only one stage-direction: "*Enter Prince, Leonato, Claudio, and Jacke Wilson.*" This shows that the folio was printed from a copy of the quarto used in the theatre, Jack Wilson probably being the singer who took the part of Balthazar. The quarto itself would appear to have been printed from a stage copy; for in iv. 2. 1 both that ed. and the folio assign the speech to "*Keeper,*" doubtless a misprint for *Kemp,* who is known to have acted the part of Dogberry. The next speech is also given by both eds. to "*Cowley,*" and another speech of Verges (iv. 2. 5) is assigned to the same actor. See also on iv. 2. 1 below.

34. *How still,* etc. Cf. *M. of V.* v. 1. 56:

"soft stillness and the night
Become the touches of sweet harmony."

38. *Kid-fox.* Young fox. Warb. changed it to "hid fox," which may be what S. wrote.

40. *Good my lord.* See Gr. 13.

41. *To slander.* For the omission of *as,* see Gr. 281.

44. *Woo.* Solicit, urge. Cf. *A. Y. L.* i. 3. 137: "Leave me alone to woo him;" *Oth.* iii. 3. 293: "Wooed me to steal it," etc.

53. *Nothing.* The reading of the early eds. changed by Theo. to "noting;" but, as W. has shown, *nothing* was then pronounced *noting,* and there is here a play on the two words, as on *Goths* and *goats* in *A. Y. L.* iii. 3. 9 (see note in our ed. p. 179). *Nothing* rhymes with *doting* in *Sonn.* 20. 12.

W. sees the same pun in the title of the play. He says: "The play is *Much Ado about Nothing* only in a very vague and general sense, but *Much Ado about Noting* in one especially apt and descriptive; for the much ado is produced entirely by noting. It begins with the noting of the Prince and Claudio, first by Antonio's man, and then by Borachio, who reveals their confidence to John; it goes on with Benedick noting the Prince, Leonato, and Claudio in the garden, and again with Beatrice noting Margaret and Ursula in the same place; the incident upon which its action turns is the noting of Borachio's interview with Margaret by

ACT II. SCENE III. 137

the Prince and Claudio; and, finally, the incident which reveals the plot is the noting of Borachio and Conrade by the Watch." *Note* = observe, watch, is common in S. Cf. *A. Y. L.* iii. 2. 267: "Slink by and note him;" *T. and C.* i. 2. 251: "Mark him, note him," etc. See also in the present play i. 1. 145, iv. 1. 156, etc.

54. *Divine air!* Probably meant to be understood as a quotation.

55. *Guts.* The word was not so offensive in the time of S. as now. See *Ham.* p. 241. Topsell, in his *Hist. of Four-footed Beasts*, 1607, stating the uses of the sheep, gives "his guts and intrals for musicke."

Hale. Draw; etymologically the same as *haul*, which S. does not use, unless, with Schmidt, we recognize a solitary instance in 2 *Hen. IV.* v. 5. 37, where the quarto has "halde" and the folio "hall'd." *Hale* is also the form in Milton (*P. L.* ii. 596) and in the A. V. (*Luke*, xii. 58, *Acts*, viii. 3). S. uses the word fifteen times; and he apparently uses *exhale* as if it were a derivative of *hale* (=draw out), as in *Rich. III.* i. 2. 58, 166, etc.

On the effect of music here, cf. *T. N.* ii. 3. 60: "a catch that will draw three souls out of one weaver."

56. *When all's done.* After all. Cf. *M. N. D.* iii. 1. 16: "I believe we must leave the killing out, when all is done." See also *T. N.* ii. 3. 31 and *Macb.* iii. 4. 67.

65. *Moe.* An old form used very often by S. but generally changed to *more* by the modern editors, unless it is necessary for the rhyme, as here and in *R. of L.* 1479. See *A. Y. L.* p. 176.

66. *Dumps.* Low spirits, melancholy; as in *T. A.* i. 1. 391, *R. and J.* iv. 5. 129, etc. It is used by S. in this sense only in the plural; but the singular is found in other writers. Cf. Harrington, *Ariosto:* "Strake them into a dumpe, and made them sad;" Hall, *Homer:* "Leaving Prince Agamemnon then in dumpe and in suspense," etc. *Dump* also meant a melancholy strain of music. Cf. *T. G. of V.* iii. 2. 85: "Tune a deploring dump." See also *R. and J.* iv. 5. 108 and *R. of L.* 1127. It was also sometimes applied to an elegy. Davies of Hereford has one entitled "A Dump upon the Death of the most noble Henrie, Earle of Pembroke."

68. *Leavy.* The regular form of the word in S. and here required by the rhyme.

76. *Bode no mischief.* The howling of a dog was deemed an ill omen. *Had as lief.* See *A. Y. L.* p. 139.

Night-raven. Either the owl, or, as some explain it, the night-heron (*Ardea nycticorax*). It is probably the same as the "night-crow" of 3 *Hen. VI.* v. 6. 45. Cf. Milton, *L'All.* 7: "And the night-raven sings;" B. J., *Poetaster:* "The dismall night-raven and tragicke owle."

83. *To-day, that.* The pointing of the early eds., followed by the Camb. editors and some others. Most of the modern eds. print "to-day? that," etc.

85. *Stalk on.* An allusion to the use of the *stalking-horse* in fowling. See *A. Y. L.* p. 199. Reed quotes John Gee's *New Shreds of the Old Snare:* "Methinks I behold the cunning fowler such as I have knowne in the fenne countries and els-where, that doe shoot at woodcockes,

snipes, and wilde fowle, by sneaking behind a painted cloth which they carrey before them, having pictured in it the shape of a horse; which while the silly fowle gazeth on, it is knockt down with hale shot, and so put in the fowler's budget."

90. *Sits the wind*, etc. Cf. *M. of V.* i. 1. 18 : "to know where sits the wind ;" *Ham.* i. 3. 56 : "The wind sits in the shoulder of your sail," etc.

91. Some point the passage thus : "I cannot tell what to think of it ; but that she loves him with an enraged affection,—it is past the infinite of thought." *Enraged* = mad, intense. *Infinite* = infinite stretch, utmost power.

97. *Came*. For the omission of the relative, see Gr. 244. *Discovers* = shows. Cf. i. 2. 10 above ; also 142 and iii. 2. 82 below.

101. *Sit you*. For *you*, see Gr. 220.

105. *Would*. Apparently used for *should*; but Abbott (Gr. 331) explains it "I was willing and prepared to think," etc.

112. *Hold it up*. Keep it up, continue it. Cf. *M. N. D.* iii. 2. 239: "hold the sweet jest up ;" *Ham.* v. 1. 34 : "they hold up Adam's profession," etc.

122. *Writ*. For the form, see *Ham.* p. 178 or Gr. 343.

128. *That*. For this affirmative use of *that*, cf. *J. C.* ii. 1. 15 : "Crown him ? That."

129. *Halfpence*. That is, pieces as small as halfpence ; but Theo. explains it as "pieces *of the same bigness*," and compares *A. Y. L.* iii. 2. 372 : "all like one another, as halfpence are." The old silver halfpenny was smaller than our half-dime.

130. *To write*. That is, *as* to write. See on 41 above.

135. *Cries*. The early eds. have "curses," which seems out of place here. *Cries* is the very plausible emendation of the Coll. MS., and is adopted by W. and H. Perhaps S. wrote "curses, prays," and the printer accidentally transposed the words.

138. *Ecstasy*. Madness, passion. See *Ham.* p. 201 or *Macb.* p. 211.

Overborne. Overcome. Cf. *M. N. D.* ii. 1. 92, *Hen. V.* iv. chor. 39, etc.

139. *Afeard*. Used by S. interchangeably with *afraid*. See *M. N. D.* p. 156 or *Macb.* p. 163.

145. *An alms*. A charity, a good deed. The Coll. MS. has "almsdeed," which W. and H. adopt ; but this use of *alms* is natural enough in itself and not without precedent in our old literature. Halliwell quotes the interlude of *The Disobedient Child*: "It were almes, by my trothe, thou were well beaten."

146. *Excellent*. An adverb, as often. Cf. iii. 1. 98 below : "an excellent good name," etc. *Exceeding* (148) is also much used in the same way. Gr. 1.

150. *Blood*. See on ii. 1. 162 above.

154. *Dotage*. Doting affection ; as in 198 below. See also *M. N. D.* iv. 1. 52, *Oth.* iv. 1. 27, *A. and C.* i. 1. 1, etc.

155. *Daffed*. The same as *doff* = *do off*. Here it means to put aside, as in v. 1. 78 below. It is used literally in *A. and C.* iv. 4. 13 :

"He that unbuckles this, till we do please
To daff 't for our repose, shall hear a storm."

ACT II. SCENE III. 139

165. *Contemptible.* Contemptuous. Cf. *medicinable*, ii. 2. 5 above. On the other hand, *contemptuous* is sometimes used in the sense of contemptible; as in 2 *Hen. VI.* i. 3. 86: "Contemptuous base-born callet as she is."

166. *Proper.* Good-looking, handsome; as in *M. N. D.* i. 2. 88, *M. of V.* i. 2. 77, etc.

167. *A good outward happiness.* "A happy exterior, a prepossessing appearance" (Schmidt). Cf. "excellent differences"=different excellencies, in *Ham.* v. 2. 112, and see note in our ed. p. 271.

168. *Fore.* See *Hen V.* p. 155.

171. *Wit.* Wisdom, intellectual power; as the connection shows. See on i. 1. 57 above, and cf. 213 below.

172. *And I take him*, etc. The quarto gives the speech to Claudio.

181. *Large.* Free, broad. Cf. iv. 1. 49 below.

185. *Counsel.* "Reflection, deliberation" (Schmidt).

189. *Let it cool the while.* Let it rest meanwhile. Cf. iii. 2. 115 below: "bear it coldly but till midnight."

191. *Unworthy.* The folio has "unworthy to have."

196. *Carry.* Carry out, manage. Cf. iv. 1. 208 below: "this well carried," etc. See also *M. N. D.* iii. 2. 240, *T. N.* iii. 4. 150, etc.

198. *And no such matter.* And it is nothing of the kind, it is not so at all. Cf. *Sonn.* 87. 14: "In sleep a king, but waking no such matter." See also i. 1. 168 above and v. 4. 82 below.

199. *Merely.* Entirely. See *Temp.* p. 111 or *J. C.* p. 129.

A dumb show. A pantomime; like that introduced in *Ham.* iii. 2 before the play, and in *Per.* at the beginning of act iii.

201. *The conference was sadly borne.* The conversation was seriously carried on. See on *sad*, i. 1. 162 above.

204. *Have their full bent.* Are at their utmost tension; a metaphor taken from the bending of a bow. Cf. *T. N.* ii. 4. 38:

"Then let thy love be younger than thyself,
Or thy affection cannot hold the bent."

205. *Censured.* Judged, estimated. Cf. *Cor.* ii. 1. 25: "do you two know how you are censured here in the city?" *J. C.* iii. 2. 16: "censure me in your wisdom, and awake your senses that you may the better judge," etc. See also on the noun in *Macb.* p. 251 or *Ham.* p. 190.

211. *Reprove.* Disprove, confute. Cf. *V. and A.* 787: "What have you urg'd that I cannot reprove?" 2 *Hen. VI.* iii. 1. 40: "Reprove my allegation, if you can."

213. *Argument.* Proof. Cf. *L. L. L.* i. 2. 175: "a great argument of falsehood," etc.

218. *Quips.* Sarcasms. Cf. *T. G. of V.* iv. 2. 12:

"all her sudden quips,
The least whereof would quell a lover's hope;"

Milton, *L'All.* 27: "Quips, and cranks, and wanton wiles," etc.

Sentences. Maxims. Cf. *R. of L.* 244: "a sentence or an old man's saw;" *M. of V.* i. 2. 11: "Good sentences," etc.

232. *Choke a daw.* The Coll. MS. has "not choke," which H. (school ed.) adopts, though not without hesitation. As the difference between

the *maximum* that would *not* choke and the *minimum* that *would* is practically *nil*, the emendation seems a most superfluous one.

Withal = with. Cf. i. 2. 18 above, where it = with *it*. For *stomach*, see on i. 3. 14 above.

239. *A Jew*. Often used in this contemptuous way. Cf. *M. of V.* ii. 2. 119: "I am a Jew if I serve the Jew any longer;" 1 *Hen. IV.* ii. 4. 198: "I am a Jew else, an Ebrew Jew," etc.

ACT III.

SCENE I.—1. *Thee.* Possibly = *thou.* See Gr. 212.

3. *Proposing.* Conversing; from the Fr. *propos*, discourse, talk (Steevens). Cf. the use of the noun in 12 just below. So *proposer* = speaker, orator, in *Ham.* ii. 2. 297.

4. *Whisper her ear.* Cf. *A. W.* ii. 3. 75: "The blushes in my cheeks thus whisper me;" *W. T.* i. 2. 437: "Your followers I will whisper to the business," etc. See Gr. 200.

7. *Pleached.* See on *thick-pleached*, i. 2. 8 above.

8. *Honeysuckles.* See *M. N. D.* p. 173.

12. *Propose.* The quarto reading; the folio has "purpose," which Reed defends as sometimes used in the same sense. He quotes Knox's *Reformation in Scotland:* "with him six persons; and getting entrie, held purpose with the porter;" and again: "After supper he held comfortable purpose of God's chosen children." *Propose* is, however, generally adopted by the editors. For *listen*, see Gr. 199.

16. *Trace.* Walk, pace. Cf. *M. N. D.* ii. 1. 25: "trace the forests wild."

24. *Lapwing.* See *Ham.* p. 272.

25. *Conference.* See on ii. 3. 202 above.

36. *Haggards.* Wild or untrained hawks. Cf. *T. of S.* iv. 1. 196:

"Another way I have to man my haggard.
To make her come and know her keeper's call;"

Id. iv. 2. 39: "this proud disdainful haggard;" *T. N.* iii. 1. 71:

"And, like the haggard, check at every feather
That comes before his eye."

In *Oth.* iii. 3. 260, the word is used as an adjective = wild, untractable.

42. *Wish.* Desire, bid. Cf. *M. for M.* v. 1. 79:

Duke. You were not bid to speak.
Lucio.   No, my good lord;
Nor wish'd to hold my peace."

For *wrestle . . . to let*, see Gr. 349.

45. *As full as fortunate.* Fully as fortunate (St., Camb. ed., and Schmidt). Most eds. point "as full, as fortunate." Both quarto and folio have "as full as."

50. *Of prouder stuff.* Cf. *J. C.* iii. 2. 97: "Ambition should be made of sterner stuff." See also *Ham.* iii. 4. 36, iv. 7. 31, etc.

51. *Disdain and scorn*, etc. Cf. *Euphues Golden Legacie*, 1590: "Her

eyes were like those lampes that make the wealthie covert of the Heavens more gorgeous, sparkling favour and disdaine, courteous and yet coye, as if in them Venus had placed all her amorets, and Diana all her chastitie."

52. *Misprising.* Slighting, despising. Cf. *A. Y. L.* i. 1. 177 : "I am altogether misprised ;" *Id.* i. 2. 192 : "your reputation shall not therefore be misprised," etc. So *misprision* — contempt in *A. W.* ii. 3. 159.

54. *Weak.* "Almost = stupid" (Schmidt). Cf. *L. L. L.* v. 2. 374: "Your wit makes wise things foolish."

55. *Project.* Idea (Schmidt).

56. *Self-endeared.* Self-loving, absorbed in love of self.

60. *How.* However. Cf. *Sonn.* 28. 8 : " How far I toil, still farther off from thee ;" *Cymb.* iv. 2. 17 : "How much the quantity, the weight as much," etc. See Gr. 46.

61. *Spell him backward.* Misconstrue him; "alluding to the practice of witches in uttering prayers" (Steevens).

63. *Black.* Dark-complexioned. Cf. *T. G. of V.* v. 2. 12 : "Black men are pearls in beauteous ladies' eyes."

Drawing of. For the *of*, see Gr. 178. An *antic* was a buffoon. See *Rich. II.* p. 192.

65. *Low.* For *low* as opposed to *tall*, cf. i. 1. 152 above. See also *M. N. D.* iii. 2. 295 fol.

An agate. Alluding to the figures cut in the agates set in rings. Cf. *L. L. L.* ii. 1. 236 : "His heart, like an agate, with your print impress'd ;" *2 Hen. IV.* i. 2. 19 : "I was never manned with an agate till now." Warb. wished to read "aglet" (the Fr. *aiguilliette*).

70. *Simpleness.* Simplicity, innocence. Cf. *M. N. D.* v. 1. 83 : "simpleness and duty ;" *A. W.* i. 1. 51 : "the better for their simpleness." In *R. and J.* iii. 3. 77 it means silliness.

71. *Commendable.* Accented on the first syllable, as regularly in S., except in *M. of V.* i. 1. 111, which Schmidt considers doubtful. Abbott (Gr. 490) also excepts *Ham.* i. 2. 87, but the other accent seems better there.

72. *Not.* Mason and Capell read "nor," and Rowe "for."

From all fashions. Averse to the ordinary ways of people. For *from* = away from, out of, cf. *Temp.* i. 1. 65 : "Which is from my remembrance ;" *J. C.* i. 3. 35 : "Clean from the purpose" (see also *Ham.* iii. 2. 22), etc. There is a play upon this sense of *from* in *M. of V.* iii. 2. 192 and *Rich. III.* iv. 4. 258.

76. *Press me to death.* Alluding to the ancient punishment of the *peine forte et dure*, or pressing to death by heavy weights laid upon the body. Cf. *M. for M.* v. 1. 528 : "pressing to death, whipping, and hanging ;" *Rich. II.* iii. 4. 72 : "I am press'd to death through want of speaking," etc.

79. *It were a better death*, etc. The reading of the quarto, which has "then," the old form of *than*. The 1st folio reads "a better death, to die ;" and the 2d folio "a bitter death to die." W. adopts this last reading, on the ground that the one in the text "can only refer to Benedick's consuming away in sighs ; whereas it is herself that Hero represents as being in danger of being pressed to death with wit, if she reveal Benedick's passion, and '*therefore*,' she says, 'let Benedick consume,' etc."

But when Hero speaks of being pressed to death with wit, it is a mere feminine hyperbole; she has of course no real fear of such a death. Her thoughts then turn to Benedick, who, like herself, would be exposed to the mocks of Beatrice if his passion became known to her; and she says, naturally enough, Better let him die of secret love than of Beatrice's scorn. The transition is as thoroughly feminine as the form of expression.

80. *Tickling*. Metrically a trisyllable, like *handling* in 2 *Hen. IV.* iv. 1. 161, *tacklings* in 3 *Hen. VI.* v. 4. 18, etc. See Gr. 477.

89. *Swift*. Ready; as in *A. Y. L.* v. 4. 65 : "he is very swift and sententious," etc.

90. *Priz'd*. Estimated; as in iv. 1. 216 below: "what we have we prize not to the worth." See also *T. and C.* iv. 4. 136, *L. L. L.* v. 2. 224, etc.

96. *Argument*. "Discourse, or the powers of reasoning" (Johnson and Schmidt).

101. *Every day, to-morrow*. "Every day after to-morrow; a play on the question" (St.)

103. *Furnish*. Dress. Cf. *A. Y. L.* iii. 2. 258: "furnished like a hunter;" *R. and J.* iv. 2. 35:

> "such needful ornaments
> As you think fit to furnish me to-morrow."

104. *Lim'd*. Ensnared as with birdlime. For the metaphor, cf. *T. N.* iii. 4. 82: "I have limed her;" *Ham.* iii. 3. 68:

> "O limed soul that, struggling to be free,
> Art more engag'd!"

See also *R. of L.* 88, *Macb.* iv. 2. 34, etc. For *lim'd* the folio has "tane."

107. *What fire is in mine ears?* Warb. sees here an allusion to the vulgar notion that the ears burn when other people are talking of us. As Reed notes, the idea is very ancient, being mentioned by Pliny. Cf. Holland's translation : "Moreover is not this an opinion generally received, That when our ears do glow and tingle, some there be that in our absence doe talke of us?" Steevens quotes *The Castell of Courtesie*, 1582 :

> "That I doe credite giue
> vnto the saying old,
> Which is, when as the eares doe burne,
> some thing on thee is told."

We are inclined to think, with Schmidt, that Beatrice does not refer to the proverb, but means simply "What fire pervades me by what I have heard!"

110. *No glory lives*, etc. "The proud and contemptuous are never extolled in their absence" (St.). The Coll. MS. reads "but in the lack."

112. *Taming*, etc. "This image is taken from falconry. She had been charged with being as wild as *haggards of the rock ;* she therefore says that, *wild* as her *heart* is, she will *tame* it *to the hand*" (Johnson)

116. *Reportingly*. On hearsay.

SCENE II.—1. *Consummate*. For the form, cf. *M. for M.* v. 1. 383 :

> "Do you the office, friar; which consummate,
> Return him here again."

See Gr. 342.

ACT III. SCENE II.

3. *Bring.* Accompany. Cf. *W. T.* iv. 3. 122: "Shall I bring thee on the way?" See also *Gen.* xviii. 16, *Acts*, xxi. 5, etc. *Vouchsafe* – allow; as in *C. of E.* v. 1. 282: "vouchsafe me speak a word," etc.

5. *The new gloss*, etc. Cf. *Macb.* i. 7. 34: "Which would be worn now in their newest gloss;" *Oth.* i. 3. 227: "the gloss of your new fortunes."

As to show a child, etc. Cf. *R. and J.* iii. 2. 29:

"As is the night before some festival
To an impatient child that hath new robes
And may not wear them."

7. *Only.* That is, only for his company. See on ii. 1. 123 above.

10. *Hangman.* Cf. *M. of V.* iv. 1. 125: "the hangman's axe;" and see note in our ed. p. 157. D. thinks it possible that *hangman* in the present passage may be = rascal, rogue, as Johnson explains it in his *Dict*. It is certain that the word, having come to mean "an executioner in general," was afterwards used as a general term of reproach. It was also used sportively in this sense, and Nares gives this passage as an instance. He also cites Heywood, 1 *Edward IV.* v. 3:

"How dost thou, Tom? and how doth Ned? quoth he;
That honest, merry hangman, how doth he?"

11. *As a bell*, etc. "A covert allusion to the old proverb, 'As the fool thinketh, so the bell clinketh'" (Steevens). *Sound as a bell* was a common expression, of which Halliwell gives many examples.

19. *The toothache.* Boswell quotes B. and F., *The False One*:

"You had best be troubled with the toothache too,
For lovers ever are."

22. *Hang it first, and draw it afterwards.* A quibbling allusion to "hanging, drawing, and quartering." Cf. *M. for M.* ii. 1. 215: "they will draw you, Master Froth, and you will hang them;" *K. John*, ii. 1. 504:

"Drawn in the flattering table of her eye!
Hang'd in the frowning wrinkle of her brow!
And quarter'd in her heart!"

24. *Worm.* A worm at the root of the tooth was formerly supposed to be the cause of toothache. Cf. Bartholomæus, *De Prop. Rerum*, 1535: "some tyme by wormes they [the teeth] ben chaunged into yelow colour, grene, or black: all this cometh of corrupt and evyll humours;" and again: "Wormes of the teethe ben slayne with myrre and opium."

25. *Can.* Pope's correction of the "cannot" of the early eds.

28. *Fancy.* Love; as often. See *M. of V.* p. 148 or *M. N. D.* p. 129. Don Pedro plays upon the word.

31. *Two countries at once.* Steevens quotes Dekker, *Seven deadly Sinnes of London*, 1606: "For an Englishman's sute is like a traitor's body that hath been hanged, drawne, and quartered, and is set up in severall places: his codpiece is in Denmarke: the collor of his dublet and the belly, in France: the wing and narrow sleeve, in Italy: the short waste hangs ouer a Dutch botcher's stall in Utrich: his huge sloppes speaks Spanish: Polonia gives him the bootes," etc.

32. *Slops.* Large loose breeches; as in the passage just quoted. Cf.

2 *Hen. IV.* i. 2. 34: "my short cloak and my slops;" *R. and J.* ii. 4. 47: "your French slop." Steevens quotes B. J., *Alchemist:*

"six great slops
Bigger than three Dutch hoys."

No doublet. M. Mason thought this should be "all doublet," to correspond with the actual dress of the old Spaniards. Steevens says: "*no doublet;* or, in other words, all cloak."

The passage *Or in the shape . . . no doublet* was omitted in the folio, probably to avoid giving offence to the Spaniards, with whom James became a friend in 1604 (Malone).

41. *Stuffed tennis balls.* Steevens cites Nash, *Wonderful Prognostication for* 1591: "they may sell their haire by the pound, to stuffe tennice balls;" and Henderson adds *Ram Alley*, 1611: "Thy beard shall serve to stuff those balls by which I get me heat at tenice;" and *The Gentle Craft*, 1600: "He 'll shave it off, and stuffe tenice balls with it."

49. *Note.* Mark, sign. Cf. *IV. T.* i. 2. 287: "a note infallible;" *Hen. V.* iv. chor. 25: "Upon his royal face there is no note," etc.

The quarto assigns this speech to "*Bene.*," the folio to "*Prin.*"

50. *To wash his face.* "That the benign effect of the tender passion upon Benedick in this regard should be so particularly noticed requires, perhaps, the remark that in Shakespeare's time our race had not abandoned itself to that reckless use of water, either for ablution or potation, which has more recently become one of its characteristic traits" (W.).

54. *A lute-string.* Love-songs were then generally sung to the music of the lute. Cf. *Hen. IV.* i. 2. 84: "a lover's lute." The *stops* of a lute were "small lengths of wire on which the fingers press the strings" (Busby). They were also called *frets.* See *Ham.* p. 230, note on *Fret.*

55. *Conclude.* The folio does not repeat the word.

60. *Conditions.* Qualities; as in *Hen. V.* iv. 1. 108, *A. W.* iv. 3. 288, etc.

62. *Face upwards.* Theo. wanted to read "heels upwards" or "face downwards," and Johnson and Steevens favoured the change; but the true interpretation is probably suggested by *W. T.* iv. 4. 131 and *Per.* v. 3. 43.

63. *Charm for the toothache.* Scot, in his *Discoverie of Witchcraft,* 1584, gives many charms for the toothache, one of which is the repeating of the following formula: "*Strigiles falcesque dentatae, dentium dolorem persanate*—O horsse-combs and sickles that have so many teeth, come heale me now of my toothach."

65. *Hobby-horses.* For the literal meaning of the word, see *Ham.* p. 225. It was used figuratively as a term of familiarity or of contempt. Cf. *L. L. L.* iii. 1. 31, *W. T.* i. 2. 276, and *Oth.* iv. 1. 160.

67. *To break with.* See on i. 1. 275 above.

72. *Good den.* Good evening. See *Hen. V.* p. 164, note on *God-den.*

82. *Discover.* Reveal. See on i. 2. 10 above.

84. *Aim better at me.* Form a better opinion of me. Cf. *T. G. of V.* iii. 1. 45: "That my discovery be not aimed at" (that is, guessed at, suspected). See also *Rich. III.* i. 3. 65 and *Ham.* iv. 5. 9.

85. *For.* As for, as regards. Gr. 149.

Holds you well. Thinks well of you. Cf. *T. and C.* ii. 3. 190: "'T is said he holds you well" (see also iv. 1. 77); *Oth.* i. 3. 396: "He holds me well."

86. *In dearness of heart.* Out of love to you. For *help*, see on i. 1. 43 above.

89. *Circumstances shortened.* Not to go into particulars. Schmidt makes it = without ceremony. Cf. *T. of S.* v. 1. 28: "To leave frivolous circumstances," etc.

90. *A talking of.* Cf. *Temp.* ii. 1. 185: "go a bat-fowling," etc. Gr. 140.

105. *Trust that you see*, etc. For the omission of the relative, especially frequent after the demonstrative *that*, see Gr. 244.

115. *Bear it coldly.* Keep quiet about it. Cf. ii. 3. 189 above: "let it cool the while." For *midnight* the folio has "night."

117. *Untowardly.* Perversely, unluckily. S. uses the word nowhere else, but he has *untoward* (= refractory, unmannerly) in *T. of S.* iv. 5. 79 and *K. John*, i. 1. 243.

SCENE III.—*Dogberry* gets his name from a shrub growing in the hedges throughout England, and *Verges* is the provincial pronunciation of *verjuice* (Steevens). Halliwell says that *Dogberry* occurs as a surname in a charter of the time of Richard II., and *Varges* as that of a usurer in *MS. Ashmol.* 38, where this epitaph is given: "Here lyes father Varges, who died to save charges."

7. *Give them their charge.* As Malone remarks, to *charge* his fellows seems to have been a regular part of the duty of the constable of the watch. Cf. Marston, *Insatiate Countess:* "Come on, my hearts: we are the city's security; I 'll give you your charge."

10. *George.* Halliwell reads "Francis," supposing him to be the person mentioned in iii. 5. 52 below; but that is not certain.

13. *Well-favoured.* Good-looking. See on *favour*, ii. 1. 81 above.

21. *Lantern.* Spelt "lanthorn" in the early eds. The sides of the lantern were then made of *horn*, and that may have suggested the orthography, though it has no connection with the etymology of the word. Cf. the quibble in *2 Hen. IV.* i. 2. 55: "he hath the horn of abundance, and the lightness of his wife shines through it." The lantern, like the *bill* and *bell*, was a part of the regular equipment of the watch. Cf. *Wit in a Constable*, 1639:

> "You 're chatting wisely o'er your bills and lanthorns,
> As becomes watchmen of discretion."

31. *No noise.* Cf. *R. and J.* i. 4. 40: "Don 's the mouse [ ] = keep still], the constable's own word."

38. *Bills.* The bill was a kind of pike or halberd, formerly the weapon of the English infantry. See *Rich. II.* p. 190. Johnson says that it was still carried by the watchmen of Lichfield in his day. Steevens quotes *Arden of Feversham*, 1592:

> "the watch
> Are coming toward our house with glaives and bills."

44. *Not the men*, etc. Halliwell says that this was the usual excuse made by the constables when they had searched innocent persons.

K

53. *They that touch pitch.* A popular proverb, found in *Ecclesiasticus*, xiii. 1 : "He that toucheth pitch shall be defiled therewith."

60. *If you hear a child cry*, etc. Steevens remarks : " It is not impossible but that part of this scene was intended as a burlesque on *The Statutes of the Streets*, imprinted by Wolfe in 1595. Among these I find the following :

'22. No man shall blowe any horne in the night, within this citie, or whistle after the hour of nyne of the clock in the night, under paine of imprisonment.

'23. No man shall use to goe with visoures, or disguised by night, under paine of imprisonment.

'24. Made that night-walkers and evisdroppers, have like punishment.

'25. No hammer-man, as a smith, a pewterer, a founder, and all artificers making great sound, shall not worke after the houre of nyne at night,' etc.

'30. No man shall, after the houre of nyne at night, keep any rule,* whereby any such suddaine outcry be made in the still of the night, as making any affray, or beating his wyfe, or servant, or singing, or revyling in his house, to the disturbaunce of his neighbours, under payne of iiis. iiiid.,' etc."

Ben Jonson is thought to have ridiculed this scene in the induction to his *Bartholomew Fair:* "And then a substantial watch to have stole in upon 'em, and taken them away with mistaking words, as the fashion is in the stage practice." Yet, as M. Mason observes, Ben himself, in his *Tale of a Tub*, makes his wise men of Finsbury speak in the same blundering style. Gifford believes it very improbable that Jonson refers to S., as these "mistaking words" were common in the plays of the time, and are elsewhere put into the mouths of constables.

69. *Present.* Represent; but not one of Dogberry's blunders. Cf. *Temp.* iv. 1. 167 : "when I presented Ceres ;" and see *M. N. D.* p. 156.

73. *Statues.* The folio reading ; the quarto has "statutes." It is impossible to decide whether the blunder is Dogberry's or the folio printer's.

78. *Keep your fellows' counsels and your own.* This is part of the oath of a grand juryman, and is one of many proofs of the poet's familiarity with legal formalities and technicalities.

85. *Coil.* Bustle, confusion. Cf. v. 2. 83 below : "yonder 's old coil at home ;" and see *M. N. D.* p. 168.

92. *Scab.* There is a play on the word, which sometimes meant a contemptible fellow. Cf. *T. N.* ii. 5. 82 : "Out, scab !" For the quibble, cf. *T. and C.* ii. 1. 31, *Cor.* i. 1. 169, and *2 Hen. IV.* iii. 2. 296.

95. *Pent-house.* A porch or shed with sloping roof, common in the domestic architecture of the time. There was one on the house in which S. was born, as is shown in the accompanying view copied from an old print.

---

* *Keep any rule* pursue any line of conduct. Cf. *night rule* in *M. N. D.* iii 2. 5, and see note in our ed. p. 160

JOHN SHAKESPEARE'S HOUSE.

96. *Like a true drunkard.* Malone suggests that S. may have called him Borachio from the Spanish *borracho*, a drunkard, or *borracha*, a leathern bottle for wine.

103. *Villany.* Warb. wished to read "villain" here; but it is natural that Borachio should repeat the word, and the use of the abstract for the concrete is a familiar rhetorical figure.

106. *Unconfirmed.* Inexperienced; as in *L. L. L.* iv. 2. 19: "his undressed, unpolished, uneducated, unpruned, untrained, or, rather, unlettered, or, ratherest, unconfirmed fashion."

115. *This seven year.* A common phrase for a long time. See on i. 1. 75 above, and cf. 1 *Hen. IV.* ii. 4. 343, etc.

120. *Bloods.* Young fellows. Cf. *J. C.* iv. 3. 262: "I know young bloods look for a time of rest." Elsewhere it means men of spirit or mettle; as in *J. C.* i. 2. 151: "the breed of noble bloods." See also *K. John*, ii. 1. 278, 461.

122. *Reechy.* Reeky, smoky, dirty. See *Ham.* p. 240.

123. *In the old church window.* That is, in the painted glass. There were threescore and ten of the *god Bel's priests*, as we learn from the *Apocrypha*.

124. *Smirched.* Smutched, soiled. Cf. iv. 1. 131 below: "smirched thus and mir'd with infamy." See also *A. Y. L.* i. 3. 114 and *Hen. V.* iii. 3. 17.

The shaven Hercules is probably the hero shaved to look like a woman while in the service of Omphale, his Lydian mistress (Steevens). Warb. thought that the reference was to *Samson* whom some Christian mythologists identified with Hercules. Sidney, in his *Defence of Poesie*, tells of having seen "Hercules painted *with his great beard* and furious face in a womans attire, spinning at Omphales commandement."

132. *Me.* See on i. 3. 53 above.

135. *Possessed.* Influenced (Schmidt). Cf. i. 1. 169 above: "possessed with a fury." In 141 just below it has much the same sense.

153. *A lock.* It was a fashion with the gallants of the time to wear a pendent lock of hair over the forehead or behind the ear, sometimes tied with ribbons, and called a *love-lock.* Fynes Moryson, in a description of the dress of Lord Mountjoy, says that his hair was "thinne on the head, where he wore it short, except a lock under his left eare, which he nourished the time of this warre [the Irish War, in 1599], and being woven up, hid it in his neck under his ruffe." When not on service he probably wore it displayed. The portrait of Edward Sackville, Earl of Dorset, painted by Vandyck, shows this lock with a large knot of ribbon at the end of it hanging under the ear on the left side. See on i. 1. 65 above, and cf. *The Return from Parnassus,* 1606:

"He whose thin fire dwells in a smoky roofe,
Must take tobacco, and must wear a lock."

157. *Masters.* In the quarto and the folio this speech and the next are both given to *Conrade.* In the folio, it reads thus: "*Conr.* Masters, neuer speake, vve charge you, let vs obey you to goe vvith vs." The correction, which is generally adopted, was made by Theo.

160. *We are like to prove,* etc. "Here is a cluster of conceits. *Commodity* was formerly, as now, the usual term for an article of merchandise. To *take up,* besides its common meaning (to *apprehend*), was the phrase for obtaining goods on credit. 'If a man is thorough with them in honest taking up,' says Falstaff [2 *Hen. IV.* i. 2. 45], 'then they must stand upon security.' *Bill* was the term both for a *single bond* and a *halberd*" (Malone). For the quibble, cf. 2 *Hen. VI.* iv. 7. 135: "My lord, when shall we go to Cheapside, and take up commodities upon our bills?"

162. *In question.* That is, subject to judicial examination (Steevens). Cf. 2 *Hen. IV.* i. 2. 68: "He that was in question for the robbery?"

SCENE IV.—6. *Rabato.* Collar, ruff. Cf. Dekker, *Guls Hornbook,* 1609: "Your stiff-necked rebatoes (that have more arches for pride to row under, than can stand under five London-bridges) durst not then," etc. Cotgrave, in his *Fr. Dict.,* as quoted by Nares, has "*Rabat*—a rebatoe for a woman's ruffe." Cf. Marston, *Scourge of Villanie:*

"Alas her soule struts round about her neck;
Her seate of sense is her rebato set."

8. *By my troth, 's not so good.* This is the reading of both quarto and folio, as in 17 just below. It is a contraction for "By my troth, it 's," etc. So *this is* is shortened into *this,* as in *Lear,* iv. 6. 187: "This' a good block" ("This a" in the folio). See Gr. 461.

12. *Tire.* Head-dress. Cf. *Sonn.* 53. 8: "And you in Grecian tires are painted new;" *T. G. of V.* iv. 4. 190: "If I had such a tire," etc.

16. *Exceeds.* For the intransitive use, cf. *Per.* ii. 3. 16: "To make some good, but others to exceed." The participle is often so used; as in *T. G. of V.* ii. 1. 100: "O exceeding puppet!"

ACT III. SCENE IV.   149

17. *Night-gown.* Dressing-gown, or "undress" gown. See *Macb.* p. 194.

In respect of = in comparison with; as in *L. L. L.* v. 2. 639: "Hector was but a Troyan in respect of this," etc.

18. *Cuts.* Schmidt defines *cut* as "a slope in a garment," whatever that may be, and compares *T. of S.* iv. 3. 90: "Here 's snip and nip and cut and slish and slash;" but it is doubtful whether it there has this technical meaning. Petruchio seems to be merely referring in a profane masculine way to the complicated cutting of the garment, which he has just said is "carv'd like an apple-tart." Immediately after, when the tailor asks, "But did you not request to have it cut?" he replies, "I bid thy master cut out the gown; but I did not bid him cut it to pieces." Perhaps this dialect of the mantua-maker is beyond the ken of the male critic.

19. *Down sleeves.* "Hanging sleeves" (Schmidt). As *side-sleeves* undoubtedly means long or hanging sleeves, Steevens reads "set with pearls down sleeves." In Laneham's *Account of Queen Elizabeth's Entertainment at Kenelworth-Castle*, 1575, the minstrel's "gown had side-sleeves down to the mid-leg." Stowe, in his *Chronicle*, describes these sleeves as worn in the time of Henry IV., some of which, he says, "hung downe to the feete, and at least to the knees, full of cuts and jagges, whereupon were made these verses:

> 'Now hath this land little neede of broomes,
> To sweepe away the filth out of the streete,
> Sen side-sleeves of pennilesse groomes
> Will it up licke be it drie or weete.'"

Side or *syde* is said to be used, in the North of England and in Scotland, in the sense of *long* when applied to garments. A *side-gown* a long one; as in the *Paston Letters:* "a short blue gown that was made of a side-gown." Cf. Fitzherbert's *Book of Husbandry:* "Theyr cotes be so syde that they be fayne to tucke them up whan they ride, as women do theyr kyrtels whan they go to the market."

W. remarks here: "The dress was made after a fashion which is illustrated in many old portraits. Beside a sleeve which fitted more or less closely to the arm and extended to the wrist, there was another, for ornament, which hung from the shoulder, wide and open." If this explanation is correct, *down sleeves* would mean the inner close sleeves, *side-sleeves* the outer loose ones.

Underborne. According to Schmidt and Halliwell, this = trimmed, or faced.

20. *Quaint.* Fanciful, or elegant. Cf. *T. of S.* iv. 3. 102: "a gown more quaint, more pleasing," etc.

29. *Saving your reverence.* "Margaret means that Hero was so prudish as to think that the mere mention of the word *husband* required an apology" (Camb. ed.).

33. *Light.* S. is fond of playing on the different senses of *light;* as here on that of light in weight and that of wanton (as in "a light woman"). Cf. *C. of E.* iii. 2. 52, *M. N. D.* iii. 2. 133, *M. of V.* iii. 2. 91, *Rich. II.* iii. 4. 86, *T. and C.* i. 3. 28, *Cymb.* v. 4. 25, etc.

39. *Light o' love.* A popular old dance tune, referred to again in *T. G. of V.* i. 2. 83 : "best sing it to the tune of 'Light o' love.'" Cf. Fletcher, *Two Noble Kinsmen:* "He gallops to the tune of 'Light o' love.'"

41. *Yea, light o' love.* The early eds. have "Ye light o' love," which Halliwell and the Camb. ed. retain. The former says that *light o' love* was a common term for a woman of light character.

42. *See.* The folio has "look." In *barns* there is a quibbling reference to *bairns* = children. Cf. *W. T.* iii. 3. 70 : "Mercy on 's, a barne ! a very pretty barne !" *A. W.* i. 3. 28 : "they say barnes are blessings."

44. *I scorn that with my heels.* A common expression, which is played upon by Lancelot in *M. of V.* ii. 2. 9 : "scorn running with thy heels."

47. *Ready.* Dressed. See *Macb.* p. 202, note on *Put on manly readiness.*

48. *For a hawk,* etc. *Heigh ho for a Husband* was the title of an old ballad. See on ii. 1. 287 above.

49. *For the letter,* etc. Referring to *ache* which was pronounced *aitch*, as explained in *Temp.* p. 119. Cf. Heywood, *Epigrammes*, 1566 :

> "*H* is worst among letters in the crosse-row ;
> For if thou find him either in thine elbow,
> In thine arm. or leg, in any degree ;
> In thine head, or teeth, or toe, or knee ;
> Into what place soever *H* may pike him.
> Wherever thou find *ache* thou shalt not like him ;"

and *Wit's Recreation*, 1640 :

> "Nor hawk, nor hound. nor horse, those hhh,
> But ach itself, 't is Brutus' bones attaches."

It was only the *noun*, however, that had this pronunciation ; the verb was pronounced and often spelt *ake*. In *V. and A.* 875 and *C. of E.* iii. 1. 58, the verb rhymes with *brake* and *sake*. The noun is of course dissyllabic in the plural, as is evident from the measure in *Temp.* i. 2. 370, *T. of A.* i. 1. 257, v. 1. 202.

50. *Turned Turk.* A proverbial expression = completely changed for the worse. Cf. *Ham.* iii. 2. 287 : "if the rest of my fortunes turn Turk with me ;" Cook, *Green's Tu Quoque:* "This it is to turn Turk, from an absolute and most compleat gentleman, to a most absurd, ridiculous, and fond lover."

52. *Trow.* That is, *I trow* = I wonder (Schmidt), or *trow ye* = think ye (Halliwell). Cf. *M. W.* i. 4. 140 : "Who's there, I trow ?" *Cymb.* i. 6. 47 : "What is the matter, trow ?" In affirmative sentences, *I trow* is often = "I dare say, certainly" (Schmidt). Cf. *Rich. II.* ii. 1. 218, 1 *Hen. IV.* ii. 1. 41, v. 1. 56, *R. and J.* i. 3. 33, etc.

55. *Gloves.* Presents of gloves were much in fashion in the time of S.

61. *Professed apprehension.* Set up for a wit ; as the answer shows.

66. *Carduus Benedictus.* The blessed thistle, or holy thistle, an annual plant from the south of Europe, which got its name from its reputation as a cure-all. It was even supposed to cure the plague, which was the highest praise that could be given to a medicine in that day. Stee-

vens quotes Cogan, *Haven of Health*, 1595: "This herbe may worthily
be called *Benedictus*, or *Omnimorbia*, that is, a salve for every sore, not
knowen to physitians of old time, but lately revealed by the speciall
providence of Almighty God." The *Vertuose Boke of Dystillacyon of the
Waters of all maner of Herbes*, 1527, says that "Water of Cardo Benedictus . . . heleth al dysseases that brenneth." Hayne, in his *Life of
Luther*, 1641, states that about 1527 Luther "fell sick of a congealing
blood about his heart," but "drinking the water of *carduus benedictus*,
he was presently helped." The plant retains little of its ancient reputation in our day; though, according to Sweringen's *Pharmaceutical
Lexicon* (Phila. 1873), it is naturalized in this country and "considered
tonic, diaphoretic, and emetic."

71. *Moral.* "That is, some secret meaning, like the moral of a fable"
(Johnson). Cf. *T. of S.* iv. 4. 79: "to expound the meaning or moral of
his signs and tokens."

80. *Eats his meat without grudging.* "And yet now, in spite of his
resolution to the contrary, he *feeds on love*, and likes his food" (Malone).

82. *Look with your eyes*, etc. "That is, direct your eyes toward the
same object, namely, a husband" (Steevens).

84. *A false gallop.* Cf. *A. Y. L.* iii. 2. 119: "the very false gallop of
verses." It is apparently = "forced gait" (1 *Hen. IV.* iii. 1. 135). See
A. Y. L. p. 171.

SCENE V.—9. *Off the matter.* Astray, away from the subject. Cf.
Cymb. i. 4. 17: "a great deal from the matter." *Off* is Capell's emendation for the "of" of the early eds.

11. *Honest as the skin between his brows.* A proverbial expression.
Cf. *Gammer Gurton's Needle*, 1575: "I am as true, I would thou knew,
as skin betwene thy brows;" Cartwright, *Ordinary*, v. 2: "I am as
honest as the skin that is between thy brows," etc.

15. *Palabras.* That is, *pocas palabras*, Spanish – few words. Cf. *T. of
S.* ind. i. 5: "Therefore paucas pallabris; let the world slide: sessa!"
Henley cites *The Spanish Tragedy:* "Pocas pallabras, milde as the
lambe." *Palabras* has become naturalized in *palaver*.

17. *Tedious.* The tediousness of constables was proverbial. Cf. B. J.,
Cynthia's Revels: "Ten constables are not so tedious."

19. *The poor duke's officers.* For the blundering transposition, cf. *M.
for M.* ii. 1. 47: "I am the poor duke's constable" (cf. 185).

23. *A thousand pound.* See on i. 1. 75 above. The folio has "times"
for *pound*.

33. *When the age*, etc. An obvious blunder for the old proverb,
"When the wine is in, the wit is out." Heywood, in his *Epigrammes*,
gives it "When ale is in, wit is out."

34. *A world to see.* "A treat to see" (Schmidt); "wonderful to see"
(Steevens); or "worth seeing" (Holt White). Cf. *T. of S.* ii. 1. 313:
"'t is a world to see How tame," etc. Baret, in his *Alvearie*, 1580, explains "It is a world to heare" by "it is a thing worthie the hearing;"
and in the *Myrrour of Good Manners comtyled in Latin*, etc.. "Est ope-
rae pretium doctos spectare colonos" is rendered ".A world it is to se

wyse tyllers of the grounde." Many other examples of the expression might be given.

35. *God's a good man.* Another proverbial expression. Steevens quotes the old morality of *Lusty Juventus:*

"He wyl say, that God is a good Man,
He can make him no better, and say the best he can :"

A Mery Geste of Robin Hoode: "For God is hold a righteous man ;" Burton, *Anat. of Melancholy:* "God is a good man, and will doe no harme," etc.

47. *Suffigance.* That is, sufficient.

54. *Examine those.* The folio reading; the quarto has "examination these." W. remarks: "The blunder in the quarto is entirely out of place in Dogberry's mouth; it is not of the sort which S. has made characteristic of his mind. Dogberry mistakes the significance of words, but never errs in the forms of speech; he is not able to discriminate between sounds that are like without being the same, but he is never at fault in grammar; and this putting of a substantive into his mouth for a verb is entirely at variance with his habit of thought, and confounds his cacology with that which is of quite another sort." It may be added that Dogberry has used the verb correctly in 44 above.

56. *Here's that,* etc. He touches his head as he speaks.

57. *Non-come.* "To a *non compos mentis*, put them out of their wits; or, perhaps, he confounds the term with *non plus*" (Malone).

ACT IV.

SCENE I.—6. *No.* We must agree with Gervinus (see p. 17 above) that the behaviour of Claudio here is "heartless." We do not know that Mr. Charles Cowden Clarke is too hard upon him when he says (*Shakespeare-Characters*, p. 306): "Claudio is a fellow of no nobleness of character, for instead of being the last, he is the first to believe his mistress guilty of infidelity towards him, and he then adopts the basest and the most brutal mode of punishment by casting her off at the very altar. Genuine love is incapable of revenge of any sort—I hold that to be a truism — still less of a concocted and refined revenge. Claudio is a scoundrel in grain." Miss Cecilia O'Brien ("Shakespeare's Young Men," in the *Westminster Review*, Oct. 1876) classes Claudio with Tybalt and Laertes. She says: "The young men of the fifth type . . . have all certain good points, but they are unbalanced men, and easily hurried into excesses through over-confidence in their own judgment. Tybalt, Claudio, and Laertes belong to this class, and they have all the same peculiarity. They are so fully persuaded of the justice and right of their own ideas that they take any means to gain their object, quite disregarding the cruelty, treachery, or meanness which they perpetrate. . . . Claudio is an accomplished and gallant gentleman, much liked by his friends, and really attached to Hero; but he is so bent on avenging his own fancied wrong, so sure that he has the right to do so, that he quite ignores the cruel injustice of condemning his bride unheard. There is no real sense of justice about any of this class; their feeling of honour is touched, and they are wild for revenge, but they do not care how unjustly they get it. There is a little touch of affectation about Claudio, not so strong as in Tybalt; but Don John talks of 'the exquisite Claudio,' and Benedick jeers at his fantastical language and the love of finery which he develops after falling in love." Of Benedick, on the other hand, she says: "Benedick tries hard to appear to have neither heart nor feeling, but they come out in spite of him. His mocking laugh dies into silence when people are in real trouble; he cannot resist trying to take Hero's part, and believes in her innocence more readily than her own father . . . It is curious with what cool contempt he treats Claudio when Beatrice makes him quarrel with him, as if there had been a lurking feeling in his mind that a weak nature was concealed under his friend's taking exterior."

12. *If either of you know*, etc. Douce remarks: "This is borrowed from our Marriage Ceremony, which (with a few slight changes in phraseology) is the same as was used in the time of Shakespeare."

21. *Some be of laughing*, etc. A quotation from the old grammars. Cf. Lyly, *Endymion*, 1591, where one of the characters exclaims "Heyho!" "What's that?" another asks; and the reply is: "An interjection, whereof some are of mourning: as *eho, vah*."

23. *Stand thee.* The *thee* is possibly=*thou*. See on iii. 1. 1 above.

29. *Render.* Give. Cf. *A. Y. L.* i. 2. 21: "What he hath taken away from thy father perforce, I will render thee again in affection," etc.

30. *Learn.* Teach. Cf. *Temp.* i. 2. 365: "For learning me your language," etc. See also *A. Y. L.* p. 141.

37. *Comes not*, etc. Is not that modest blush the evidence of artless innocence?

41. *Luxurious.* Lustful; as in *Macb.* iv. 3. 58, etc. It is the only sense in which S. uses either the adjective or the noun. See *Hen. V.* p. 166, note on *Luxury*.

44. *Knit.* Cf. *M. N. D.* i. 1. 172: "By that which knitteth souls and prospers loves;" *Cymb.* ii. 3. 122: "to knit their souls," etc.

Approved. See on ii. 1. 340 above.

45. *In your own proof.* In your own trial of her (Tyrwhitt).

47. *Defeat.* Ruin, destruction. Cf. *Hen. V.* i. 2. 107: "Making defeat on the full power of France;" *Ham.* ii. 2. 598:

"Upon whose property and most dear life
A damn'd defeat was made."

49. *Large.* Free, licentious. Cf. ii. 3. 181 above: "large jests."

53. *Out on thy seeming!* The old eds. have "Out on thee seeming, I will," etc. K. and V. have "Out on the seeming!" W. gives "Out on thee! Seeming!" The reading in the text was suggested by Pope, and is adopted by D., H., Halliwell, and others.

I will write against it, etc. Cf. *Cymb.* ii. 5. 32:

"I 'll write against them,
Detest them, curse them."

55. *As is the bud.* "Before the air has tasted its sweetness" (Johnson).

58. *Rage.* The Coll. MS. has "range," and in the next line "wild" for *wide*. On the latter word, cf. *T. and C.* iii. 1. 97, *Lear*, iv. 7. 50, etc.

61. *Gone about.* Endeavoured. Cf. i. 3. 11 above.

62. *Stale.* See on ii. 2. 23 above.

63. *Are these things*, etc. Cf. *Macb.* i. 3. 83: "Were such things here as we do speak about?"

65. *Nuptial.* S. uses only the singular in this sense, except in *Per.* v. 3. 80. See *Temp.* p. 143, and cf. *J. C.* p. 183, note on *His funerals*.

True! O God! This certainly refers to what Don John has just said. Some eds. print "True, O God!" as if it were a reply to Benedick; and perhaps it is.

70. *Move one question.* Cf. *T. and C.* ii. 3. 89: "We dare not move the question of our place."

71. *Kindly.* Natural. Cf. 2 *Hen. IV.* iv. 5. 84: "kindly tears," etc. In *A. and C.* ii. 5. 78, "kindly creatures" = such as the land naturally produces. Cf. "kindly fruits of the earth" in the *Prayer-Book*.

89. *Liberal.* Licentious. See *Ham.* p. 258.

90. *Encounters.* Meetings; as in iii. 3. 136 above. See also *Temp.* iii. 1. 74, v. 1. 154, etc.

93. *Spoke.* We have had *spoken* in 63 above. Gr. 343.

96. *Misgovernment.* Want of self-control, misconduct. S. uses the word only here, but he has *misgoverning* in the same sense in *R. of L.* 654.

On *thy much*, cf. *M. for M.* v. 1. 534: "thy much goodness," etc. See also *Matt.* vi. 7.

97. *What a Hero*, etc. Johnson says: "I am afraid here is intended a poor conceit upon the word *Hero*;" but, as Halliwell remarks, this is very improbable.

103. *Conjecture.* Suspicion. Cf. *W. T.* ii. 1. 176: "as gross as ever touch'd conjecture;" *Ham.* iv. 5. 15:

"she may strew
Dangerous conjectures in ill-breeding minds."

105. *Gracious.* Lovely, attractive; as in *T. N.* i. 5. 281, *K. John*, iii. 4. 81, 96, etc. The word is here a trisyllable. Gr. 479.

109. *Smother her spirits up.* Cf. *Hen. V.* iv. 5. 20: "To smother up the English," etc.

114. *May.* Can. See on ii. 3. 19 above, and cf. iii. 2. 103: "May this be so?"

120. *The story*, etc. "That is, the story which her blushes discover to be true" (Johnson). Schmidt takes *blood* to be used in the same sense as in ii. 1. 162 above. Seymour objects to the former explanation that Hero had fainted; but we find the Friar afterwards referring to the "thousand blushing apparitions" he had noted in her face, and this may be a similar reference.

123. *Spirits.* Monosyllabic, as often. Gr. 463.

124. *On the rearward.* Cf. *Sonn.* 90. 6: "In the rearward of a conquer'd woe." See also 2 *Hen. IV.* iii. 2. 339.

ACT IV. SCENE I.   155

126. *Chid.* Similarly followed by *at* in *T. G. of V.* ii. 1. 78, *A. Y. L.* iii. 5. 129, *W. T.* iv. 4. 6, etc. Elsewhere it is followed by *with*; as in *Sonn.* 111. 1, *Oth.* iv 2. 167, and *Cymb.* v. 4. 32.

Frame. "Order, disposition of things" (Steevens). Schmidt, less happily, makes *frame* mould (as in *W. T.* ii. 3. 103), and explains the passage, "Did I grumble against the niggardness of nature's casting-mould?"

127. *One too much by thee.* Cf. *T. G. of V.* v. 4. 52: "too much by one."

131. *Who smirched.* Who being smirched, if she were smirched. See Gr. 377. For *smirched* (cf. iii. 3. 124 above) the folio has "smeered."

Mir'd. Soiled. Used again as a verb (=sink in mud) in *T. of A.* iv. 3. 147: "Paint till a horse may mire upon your face." Halliwell cites Palsgrave, *Lesclarcissement de la Langue Francoyse*, 1530: "I myar, I beraye with myar; the poore man is myred up to the knees;" and Taylor, *Workes*, 1630:

> "I was well entred (forty winters since)
> As farre as *possum* in my *Accidence*;
> And reading but from *possum* to *posset*,
> There was I mir'd, and could no further get."

134. *And mine I lov'd*, etc. Warb. strangely wanted to read "as mine I lov'd, as mine I prais'd, As mine," etc. For the ellipsis of the relative, see Gr. 244; and for *on=of*, Gr. 181.

137. *Valuing of her.* "Estimating what she was to me" (Schmidt).

138. *That.* So that. Gr. 283. On the passage, cf. *Macb.* ii. 6. 60:

> "Will all great Neptune's ocean wash this blood
> Clean from my hand?"

140. *Season.* For the metaphor, cf. *A. W.* i. 1. 55: "'T is the best brine a maiden can season her praise in;" *T. N.* i. 1. 30:

> "all this to season
> A brother's dead love, which she would keep fresh
> And lasting in her sad remembrance;"

R. and J. ii. 3. 72:

> "How much salt water thrown away in waste,
> To season love, that of it doth not taste!"

See also *L. C.* 18.

142. *Attir'd in wonder.* Cf. *R. of L.* 1601: "Why art thou thus attir'd in discontent?" *T. N.* iv. 3. 3: "'t is wonder that enwraps me thus."

150. *Two.* Omitted in the folio.

152. *Wash'd.* That is, *he* washed. For the ellipsis, see Gr. 399.

153. *Hear me*, etc. In the early eds. this and the three following lines are printed as prose, and "been silent" (first transposed by W.) is given for our *silent been*. Other emendations have been suggested, but seem to be unnecessary.

154. *And given way*, etc. And let these things take their course.

155. *By noting.* From noting; because I have been noting or observing. Gr. 146.

157. *Apparitions.* Metrically equivalent to five syllables. Gr. 479.

158. *Shames.* For the plural, cf. *A. and C.* i. 4. 72:

"Let his shames quickly
Drive him to Rome."

159. *Bear.* The folio reading, and preferable to the "beate" of the quarto; though Coll. and V. adopt the latter.

161. *To burn the errors.* Steevens compares *R. and J.* i. 2. 93:

"When the devout religion of mine eye
Maintains such falsehood, then turn tears to fires;
And these, who often drown'd could never die,
Transparent heretics, be burnt for liars!"

164. *Doth warrant,* etc. That is, confirm what I have read.

166. *Reverence, calling.* The Coll. MS. gives "reverend calling," which is plausible, but no change is really required.

168. *Biting.* Often used metaphorically by S. Cf. *M. W.* v. 5. 178: 'a biting affliction;" *M. for M.* i. 3. 19: "most biting laws," etc. The Coll. MS. substitutes "blighting."

171. *Not denies.* Cf. *Temp.* ii. 1. 121: "I not doubt;" *Id.* v. 1. 38: "Whereof the ewe not bites," etc. See also v. 1. 22 below: "they themselves not feel." Gr. 305.

174. *What man,* etc. Warb. sees great subtlety in this question. No man's name had been mentioned; but had Hero been guilty it was very probable that she would not have observed this, and might therefore have betrayed herself by giving the name. We suspect, however, that there is more of Warburton than of Shakespeare in this explanation.

183. *Misprision.* Misapprehension, mistake. Cf. *M. N. D.* iii. 2. 90:

"Of thy misprision must perforce ensue
Some true love turn'd, and not a false turn'd true."

184. *The very bent of honour.* The utmost degree of honour (Johnson). Cf. ii. 3. 204 above: "her affections have their full bent;" and see note. Schmidt makes *bent* here=inclination, disposition (as in *R. and J.* ii. 2. 143, *J. C.* ii. 1. 210, etc.), but the other meaning is more appropriate and more forcible.

185. *Wisdoms.* A common use of the plural in S. See *Rich. II.* p. 206, note on *Sights*; or *Macb.* p. 209, note on *Loves.*

186. *Practice.* Plotting, trickery; as in *M. for M.* v. 1. 107, 123, 239, etc. See also *Ham.* p. 255 or *A. Y. L.* p. 156. Walker puts this among the passages in which *live* and *lie* were probably confounded by the old printers.

187. *Frame.* Framing, devising. The Coll. MS. has "fraud and."

192. *Ent.* For the form, see *Rich. II.* p. 104 or *A. Y. L.* p. 165. Gr. 343.

Invention. Mental activity (Schmidt); as in *Oth.* iv. 1. 201: "of so high and plenteous wit and invention," etc. The word is here a quadrisyllable. See on *apparitions,* 157 above.

195. *In such a kind.* Cf. ii. 1. 58 above: "in that kind." For *kind* Walker suggested "cause," which the Coll. MS. also gives. The rhyme makes *kind* suspicious.

198. *To quit me of them.* To requite myself in respect of them, to be even with them. Cf. *Cor.* iv. 5. 89: "To be full quit of those my banishers;" *T. of S.* iii. 1. 92: "Hortensio will be quit with thee," etc. See also *Rich. II.* p. 208 or *Ham.* p. 269.

ACT IV. SCENE I.

Throughly. Thoroughly. Cf. *Temp.* iii. 3. 14, *Ham.* iv. 5. 136, etc. See *M. of V.* p. 144, note on *Throughfares.*

200. *Princes.* The early eds. have "the Princesse (left for dead)." The correction is due to Theo.

203. *Ostentation.* Similarly used of funeral pomp in *Ham.* iv. 5. 215. Elsewhere it is = outward show, without the idea of pretentiousness. Cf. 2 *Hen. IV.* ii. 2. 54: "all ostentation of sorrow;" *A. and C.* iii. 6. 52:

> "The ostentation of our love, which, left unshown,
> Is often left unlov'd," etc.

In *L. L. L.* v. 2. 409 ("full of maggot ostentation") it has its modern meaning.

204. For the old custom which is here alluded to, see on v. 1. 269 below.

207. *What shall become,* etc. That is, what shall come, etc. Cf. *T. N.* ii. 2. 37: "What will become of this?" (that is, what will be the result of this?), etc.

208. *Well carried.* Cf. *M. N. D.* iii. 2. 240: "This sport, well carried, shall be chronicled." See on *carry,* ii. 3. 196 above.

209. *Remorse.* Pity. See *M. of V.* p. 156 or *Macb.* p. 171.

217. *Whiles.* Used interchangeably with *while* as a conjunction, but never as a noun. Gr. 137. The Coll. MS. transposes *lack'd* and *lost;* but *lack'd* does not mean missed, but missing, wanting. Cf. *M. of V.* i. 1. 37, *M. N. D.* ii. 1. 223, etc. Even if it were a case of what the rhetoricians call "hysteron-proteron" (a figure recognized by Puttenham in his *Arte of English Poesie,* 1589), other examples are to be found in S.

218. *Rack.* Stretch, strain, exaggerate. Cf. *M. of V.* i. 1. 181:

> "Try what my credit can in Venice do;
> That shall be rack'd even to the uttermost," etc.

221. *Upon.* In consequence of (Schmidt). Cf. v. 1. 235 below: "And fled he is upon this villany." Gr. 191.

222. *Idea.* Image. Cf. *Rich. III.* iii. 7. 13:

> "Withal I did infer your lineaments,
> Being the right idea of your father;"

L. L. L. iv. 2. 69: "forms, figures, shapes, objects, ideas," etc. S. uses the word only three times.

223. *Study.* Schmidt takes this to be a figurative use of *study* = a room for study, and compares *Sonn.* 24. 7: "my bosom's shop;" but *study of imagination* may be simply = imaginative study, imaginative reflections.

226. *Moving, delicate.* So in the early eds.; but some modern ones give "moving-delicate." Cf. Gr. 2.

227. *Eye and prospect.* Cf. *K. John.* ii. 1. 208: "Before the eye and prospect of your town."

229. *Liver.* Anciently supposed to be the seat of love. Cf. *R. of L.* 47, *Temp.* iv. 1. 56, *M. W.* ii. 1. 121, *A. Y. L.* iii. 2. 443, *T. N.* ii. 4. 101, ii. 5. 106, etc.

231. *No, though he thought,* etc. "A line instinct with touching knowledge of human charity. Pity attends the faults of the dead; and survivors visit sin with regret rather than reproach" (Clarke).

232. *Success.* That which is to *succeed* or follow, the issue. Cf. *A. and C.* iii. 5. 6: "What is the success?" 2 *Hen. VI.* ii. 2. 46: "things ill-got had ever bad success;" *T. and C.* ii. 2. 117: "bad success in a bad cause," etc.

235. *Levell'd.* Technically = aimed; as in *L. C.* 282, *Rich. III.* iv. 4. 202, etc.

238. *Sort.* Fall out, result. Cf. v. 4. 7 below: "all things sort so well." See also *M. N. D.* iii. 2. 352, *Ham.* i. 1. 109, etc.

240. *Reclusive.* Used by S. nowhere else.

242. *Advise.* That is, prevail upon by advice, persuade. Cf. *Lear*, v, 1. 2: "he is advis'd by aught," etc. See also *M. N. D.* p. 126, note on *Be advis'd.*

243. *Inwardness.* Confidence, intimacy. The noun is used by S. only here, but we have *inward* = confidential in *L. L. L.* v. 1. 102: "what is inward between us," etc. Cf. *Rich. III.* iii. 4. 8: "inward with the royal duke." So the noun *inward* = confidential friend in *M. for M.* iii. 2. 138: "I was an inward of his."

247. *Being that.* Since. Cf. 2 *Hen. IV.* ii. 1. 199: "being you are to take soldiers," etc. Gr. 378.

248. *The smallest twine*, etc. Johnson remarks: "This is one of our author's observations upon life. Men overpowered with distress eagerly listen to the first offers of relief, close with every scheme, and believe every promise. He that has no longer any confidence in himself is glad to repose his trust in any other that will undertake to guide him."

249. *Presently.* See on i. 1. 74 above.

250. *To strange sores,* etc. Cf. *Ham.* iv. iii. 9:

> "diseases desperate grown
> By desperate appliance are relieved,
> Or not at all."

261. *Even.* Plain. Cf. 2 *Hen. IV.* ii. 3. 2: "Give even way unto my rough affairs."

262. *May.* Can. See on ii. 3. 19 above.

270. *By my sword.* On swearing by the sword, see *Ham.* p. 197.

271. *By it.* These words are in the folio, but not in the quarto.

274. *Eat your word.* Cf. *A. Y. L.* v. 4. 155 and the play upon the phrase in 2 *Hen. IV.* ii. 2. 149.

287. *To deny it.* By refusing it. For the "indefinite use" of the infinitive, see Gr. 356.

289. *I am gone, though I am here.* As Beatrice is about to go, Benedick seizes and detains her; she tries in vain to escape, and says "My heart is absent, though I am present in body." As Halliwell remarks, this is very effective on the stage.

297. *Approved.* Proved. See on ii. 1. 340 above.

In the height. In the highest degree. Cf. *C. of E.* v. 1. 200: "Even in the strength and height of injury." So *to the height* and *at the height;* as in *Hen. VIII.* i. 2. 214: "to the height a traitor;" *A. Y. L.* v. 2. 50: "at the height of heart-heaviness," etc.

299. *Bear her in hand.* Keep her in expectation, flatter her with false hopes. Cf. *T. of S.* iv. 2. 3, *Macb.* iii. 1. So, *Ham.* ii. 2. 67, *Cymb.* v. 5. 43, etc.

302. *I would eat*, etc. Steevens quotes Chapman, *Iliad*, xxii. :

> "Hunger for slaughter, and a hate that eates thy heart to eate
> Thy foe's heart."

So Hecuba (*Iliad*, xxiv.), speaking of Achilles, expresses a wish to use her teeth on his liver.

304. *Proper.* Often used in this ironical way. See *Macb.* p. 218, note on *O proper stuff.* Cf. i. 3. 46 above: "A proper squire!"

310. *Counties.* See on ii. 1. 170 above.

311. *Count, Count Comfect.* The quarto reads "counte, counte comfect;" the folio, "Counte, comfect." *Count Comfect* is used in derision, like "My Lord Lollipop" (St.). W. sees a play upon both *count* and *confect.* "Her wit and her anger working together, she at once calls Claudio's accusation 'a goodly *conte* confect,' that is, a story made up, and him a *count* confect,' that is, a nobleman of sugar candy; for he was plainly a pretty fellow and a dandy; and then she clenches the nail that she has driven home by adding 'a sweet gallant, surely!' This sense of the passage . . . is further evident from the inter-dependence of the whole exclamation, 'Surely a princely *testimony*, a goodly *count*,'— the first part of which would be strangely out of place if there were no pun in the second. In Shakespeare's time the French title *Count* was pronounced like *conte* or *compte*, meaning a fictitious story, a word which was then in common use."

314. *Courtesies.* Mere forms of courtesy. Here both quarto and folio have "cursies," which Halliwell believes to be an old form used only in the sense of obeisance, or the outward manifestation of courtesy. See on ii. 1. 45 above. The *curtsy* was formerly used by men as well as women. Cf. *Rich. III.* i. 3. 49: "Duck with French nods and apish courtesy;" *L. L. L.* i. 2. 66: "a new-devised courtesy;" *A. W.* v. 3. 324: "Let thy courtesies alone; they are scurvy ones," etc.

315. *Trim.* The word, like *proper* (see on 304 above) is often used ironically. Cf. *L. L. L.* v. 2. 363: "Trim gallants;" *M. N. D.* iii. 2. 157: "A trim exploit," etc. *Ones*=tongues; such change from singular to plural being not uncommon in Elizabethan English. Cf. *Sonn.* 78. 3:

> "As every alien pen hath got my use,
> And under thee their poesie disperse;"

where the plural in *their* and in the subject of *disperse* is implied in *every pen*.

325. *Engaged.* Pledged; that is, to challenge him.

SCENE II.—*Enter . . . in gowns.* The gowns of constables are often alluded to in writers of the time. Malone quotes *The Blacke Booke*, 1604: "when they mist their constable, and sawe the blacke gowne of his office lye full in a puddle."

1. This speech is assigned to "*Keeper*" in the early eds. (see on ii. 3. 32 above), and "*Kemp*" is prefixed to most of the speeches of Dogberry in the remainder of the scene, as "*Cowley*" or "*Couley*" is to those of Verges. In line 4, however, we find "*Andrew*," a name that cannot be identified with that of any comic actor of the time; but perhaps, as Halliwell suggests, it was the familiar appellation of some one of them.

5. *Exhibition to examine.* A blunder for "examination to exhibit" (Steevens).

16-19. *Yea sir ... such villains.* Found in the quarto, but omitted in the folio. As Theo., who restored the passage to the text, remarks, "it supplies a defect, for without it the town-clerk asks a question of the prisoners, and goes on without staying for any answer to it." Blackstone believes that the omission was made on account of the statute of James I. forbidding the use of the name of God on the stage.

18. *Defend.* Forbid. See on ii. 1. 81 above.

23. *I will go about with him.* "I will go to work with him, he shall find his match in me" (Schmidt). See on i. 3. 11 above.

28. *They are both in a tale.* "They both say the same" (Schmidt). "Dogberry had heard of getting at the truth by separate examination, and sagaciously asking a question to which they could not but both give the same answer, expresses his surprise at the failure of his wise experiment. The humour of the observation is admirable" (Pye).

32. *Eftest.* Quickest, readiest (Boswell). Theo. changed it to "deftest," and Steevens thought that it was meant to be a blunder for that word. *Deftly* occurs in *Macb.* iv. 1. 68.

46. *By the mass.* Halliwell remarks that this oath was then going out of fashion, and is therefore appropriately put into the mouth of Verges — "a good old man, sir." Cf. Sir John Harrington, *Epigrams*, 1633:

> "In elder times an ancient custome was,
> To sweare in weighty matters by the Masse;
> But when the Masse went downe (as old men note)
> They swore then by the crosse of this same grote;
> And when the Crosse was likewise held in scorne,
> Then, by their faith, the common oath was sworne.
> Last, having sworne away all faith and troth,
> Onely God-damne them is their common oath.
> Thus custome kept decorum by gradation,
> That losing Masse, Crosse, Faith, they find damnation."

58. *Upon.* In consequence of. See on iv. 1. 221 above.

62. *Let them*, etc. The quarto reads: "*Couley.* Let them be in the hands of coxcombe." The folio has "*Sex.* Let them be in the hands of *Coxcombe.*" Theo. retained the old text, but gave the speech to Conrade, as W. does. The reading in our text is Malone's, who also suggested

> "*Verges.* Let them be in the hands of—
> *Conrade.* Coxcomb!"

There is not much to choose between these two emendations. The Camb. editors suggest that *Let them be in the hands* "may be the corruption of a stage-direction [*Let them bind them*] or [*Let them bind their hands*]." The Coll. MS. gives

> "*Verges.* Let them be bound.
> *Conrade.* Hands off, coxcomb!"

66. *Naughty.* Formerly used in a much stronger sense than at present. See *M. of V.* p. 152.

69. *My years.* Mr. Weiss (see p. 26 above), in quoting this passage

gives "my ears," but as we can find no authority for that reading, we take it to be a misprint; Dogberry could hardly have confounded words so familiar as *years* and *ears*.

75. *Piece of flesh*. Cf. *A. Y. L.* iii. 2. 68: "a good piece of flesh indeed!" *T. N.* i. 5. 30: "as witty a piece of Eve's flesh as any in Illyria;" *L. L. L.* iii. 1. 136: "My sweet ounce of man's flesh!"

77. *Losses*. The Coll. MS. has "leases," and some one has suggested "law-suits." These critics do not see the humour of making Dogberry boast of his "losses" as well as his "riches."

ACT V.

SCENE I.—7. *Comforter*. The quarto reading. The 1st folio has "comfort," changed in the 2d into "comfort els."

7. *Suit*. Agree, coincide. Cf. *T. N.* i. 2. 50:

"I will believe thou hast a mind that suits
With this thy fair and outward character."

10. Hanmer reads "speak to me." *Patience* is a trisyllable, as in 19 and 256 below. Gr. 479.

12. *Strain*. Feeling (Schmidt). Cf. *Sonn.* 90. 13: "strains of woe;" *T. and C.* ii. 2. 154:

"Can it be
That so degenerate a strain as this
Should once set footing in your generous bosoms?"

See also *Cor.* v. 3. 149, *T. of A.* iv. 3. 213, etc.

16. *Bid sorrow wag*, etc. This is the great *crux* of the play. The quarto and folio read: "And, sorrow, wagge, crie hem," etc. Capell's emendation in the text is perhaps as satisfactory as any that has been proposed, and is adopted by St., D., H., the Camb. editors, and others. Among the others are "And sorrow wage; cry hem" (Theo.); "And sorrow waive; cry hem" (Hanmer); "And 'sorrow, wag,' cry; hem, when" (Johnson); "Cry, 'sorrow, wag;' and hem" (also suggested by Johnson, and adopted by Steevens); "In sorrow wag; cry hem" (Malone); "And—sorrow wag!—cry hem" (D.); "Call sorrow joy, cry hem" (Coll. MS.); "And sorrowing, cry hem" (Heath, followed by Halliwell); "And sorrow's wag, cry hem" (W.), etc. Schmidt thinks that the old reading may be explained thus: "and if sorrow, a merry droll, will cry hem," etc. For *wag*=begone, cf. *M. W.* i. 3. 7: "let them wag; trot, trot." See also *Id.* ii. 1. 238, ii. 3. 74, 101; and cf. *T. A.* v. 2. 87:

"For well I wot the empress never wags
But in her company there is a Moor."

See also *Ham.* pp. 235, 265.

18. *Candle-wasters*. Those who sit up late, "burning the midnight oil;" but whether in revelry, as Steevens explains it, or in study, as Whalley suggests, has been matter of dispute. St. and D. adopt the former interpretation; but Schmidt favours the latter, making the passage—

"drown grief with the wise saws of pedants and book-worms." Ingleby also explains it, "drown one's troubles in study." Whalley quotes B. J., *Cynthia's Revels*, iii. 2: "Spoiled by a whoreson book-worm, a candle-waster." *Lamp-wasters* is similarly used in *The Antiquary*, iii.

23. *Passion*. Emotion, sorrow. Cf. *Temp*. i. 2. 392: "Allaying both their fury and my passion;" *L. L. L.* v. 2. 118: "passion's solemn tears," *T. A.* i. 1. 106: "A mother's tears in passion for her son," etc.

24. *Preceptial medicine*. The medicine of precept or counsel. Cf. i. 3. 11 above: "a moral medicine."

28. *Wring*. Writhe; as in *Hen. V*. iv. 1. 253:
"Whose sense no more can feel
But his own wringing;"
and *Cymb*. iii. 6. 79: "He wrings at some distress."

30. *Moral*. Ready to moralize. Cf. *Lear*, iv. 2. 58: 'a moral fool." Schmidt makes it an adjective with this sense in *A. Y. L.* ii. 7. 29:
"When I did hear
The motley fool thus moral on the time;"
but it is more likely a verb=moralize.

32. *Advertisement*. Admonition, moral instruction (Johnson). Cf. *A. W.* iv. 3. 240: "that is an advertisement to a proper maid in Florence, one Diana, to take heed;" 1 *Hen. IV*. iv. 1. 36: "Yet doth he give us bold advertisement." See also Baret, *Alvearie*, 1580: "A warning and admonition, an advertisement, a counsaile, an advisement or instruction, *admonitio*." So the verb=counsel, instruct; as in *M. for M*. i. 1. 42, v. 1. 388, and *Hen. VIII*. ii. 4. 178. Seymour explains the present passage: "my griefs are too violent to be expressed in words."

37. *The style of gods*. Warb. thought this referred to "the extravagant titles the stoics gave their wise men;" but, as Steevens remarks, it means simply "an exalted language, such as we may suppose would be written by beings superior to human calamities." Cf. B. and F., *Four Plays in One*:
"Athens doth make women philosophers,
And sure their children chat the talk of gods."

38. *Push*. Rowe changed this to "pish," and Schmidt makes it an interjection="pshaw, pish;" as in *T. of A*. iii. 6. 119: "Push! did you see my cap?" Boswell considers *made a push at*=contended against, defied; and cites from L'Estrange, "Away he goes, makes his push, stands the shock of battle," etc. Cf. *push*=onset, attack, in *J. C.* v. 2. 5: "And sudden push gives them the overthrow," etc.

Sufferance=suffering; as in *Sonn*. 58. 7, *M. W*. iv. 2. 2, 2 *Hen. IV*. v. 4. 28, *T. and C.* i. 1. 28, etc.

46. *Good den*. See on iii. 2. 72 above.

55. *Beshrew*. A mild form of imprecation. See *M. N. D.* p. 152.

58. *Fleer*. Grin, sneer. Palsgrave defines it thus: "I fleere, I make an yvell countenaunce with the mouthe by uncoveryng of the tethe." Cf. *R. and J.* i. 5. 59: "To fleer and scorn at our solemnity." See also *L. L. L.* v. 2. 109 and *J. C.* i. 3. 117.

62. *To thy head*. Forby, in his *East Anglian Vocabulary*, says: "We say, I told him so to his *head*, not to his face, which is the usual phrase:"

64. *Reverence*. That is, the "privilege of age" mentioned just above.

65. *Bruise of many days.* Cf. 2 *Hen. IV.* iv. 1. 100: "the bruises of the days before."

66. *Trial of a man.* Manly combat. For *trial* in this sense, cf. *Rich. II.* i. 1. 81, 151, i. 3. 99, iv. 1. 56, 71, 90, 106, etc.

71. *Fram'd.* Devised, fabricated. Cf. the use of the noun in iv. 1. 187 above.

75. *Fence.* Skill in fencing; as in 84 just below. In 3 *Hen. VI.* iv. 1. 44 ("fence impregnable") it means defence. Cf. the use of the verb defend, in *Id.* iii. 3. 98: "fence the right."

76. *May of youth.* Cf. *Hen. V.* i. 2. 120: "the very May-morn of his youth."

Lustihood. Spirit, vigour. Cf. *T. and C.* ii. 2. 50: "lustihood deject." See also Spenser. *F. Q.* iii. 10. 45: "All day they daunced with great lusty-hedd;" *Shep. Kal. May:* "In lustihede and wanton meryment;" *Muiopotmos,* 61: "Yong Clarion, with vauntfull lustie-head," etc.

77. *Away! I will not have to do with you.* Here again Claudio's behaviour is unfeeling. "The prince, who is only an acquaintance of the father Leonato, and his brother Antonio, nevertheless manifests a gentlemanly consideration and even tenderness in their family disaster; but Claudio is wholly untouched by the anguish of the old men at the loss of their child (she his own mistress too!) and at the stain upon their house. He has no word of sympathy or commiseration; he wraps himself up in contempt of their aged and feeble defiance; and immediately after they have gone out, upon Benedick's entering, he jests upon the danger that he and the prince have escaped of having their 'noses snapped off with two old men without teeth'" (Clarke).

78. *Duff.* Put off, put aside. See on ii. 3. 155 above.

80. *He shall kill,* etc. "This *brother Antony* is the truest picture imaginable of human nature. He had assumed the character of a sage to comfort his brother, overwhelmed with grief for his only daughter's affront and dishonour; and had severely reproved him for not commanding his passion better on so trying an occasion. Yet, immediately after this, no sooner does he begin to suspect that his *age* and *valour* are slighted, but he falls into the most intemperate fit of rage himself.... This is copying nature with a penetration and exactness of judgment peculiar to Shakespeare" (Warb.).

82. *Win me and wear me.* "Proverbial = let him laugh that wins; originally = win me and have or enjoy me" (Schmidt). Cf. *Hen. V.* v. 2. 250: "thou hast me, if thou hast me, at the worst; and thou shalt wear me, if thou wear me, better and better," etc. See also ii. 1. 294 above.

83. *Come, sir boy, come, follow.* The reading of the early eds. Pope changed it to "come, boy, follow."

84. *Foining.* "A term in fencing = thrusting" (Douce). Cf. *M. W.* ii. 3. 24: "To see thee fight, to see thee foin." See also 2 *Hen. IV.* ii. 1. 17 and ii. 4. 252. We have *foin* as a noun (= thrust) in *Lear,* iv. 6. 251. So in Cotgrave's *Fr. Dict.:* "*Coup d'estoc,* a thrust, foine, stockado, stab." Halliwell quotes Harrington, *Ariosto,* 1591: "Rogero never foyned, and seldome strake but flatling."

87. *Content yourself.* "Compose yourself, keep your temper" (Schmidt); as in *T. of S.* i. 1. 90, 203, ii. 1. 343, *T. and C.* iii. 2. 151, etc.

91. *Jacks.* Often used as a term of contempt. Cf. *M. of V.* iii. 4. 77: "these bragging Jacks;" 1 *Hen. IV.* iii. 3. 99: "the prince is a Jack, a sneak-cup," etc. See also i. 1. 162 above.

94. *Scambling.* Scrambling. Cf. *Hen. V.* i. 1. 4, v. 2. 218, etc.

Outfacing. "Facing the matter out with looks" (Schmidt). Cf. *A. Y. L.* i. 3. 124:

> "As many other mannish cowards have
> That do outface it with their semblances."

Fashion-monging. Foppish. It is the reading of both quarto and folio, changed in the later folios to "fashion-mongring." We have *fashion-monger* in *K. of J.* ii. 4. 34. Halliwell cites Wilson, *Coblers Prophecie,* 1594: "the money-monging mate with all his knaverie."

95. *Cog.* "To deceive, especially by smooth lies" (Schmidt). Cf. *M. W.* iii. 3. 76: "I cannot cog, and say thou art this and that, like a many of these lisping hawthorn-buds, that come like women in men's apparel," etc. See also *Rich. III.* i. 3. 48, *T. and C.* v. 6. 11, *T. of A.* v. 1. 98, etc.

Flout. See on i. 1. 162 above.

Deprave. Slander. Cf. *T. of A.* i. 2. 145: "Who lives that's not depraved or depraves?" So *depravation* = detraction in *T. and C.* v. 2. 132.

96. *Anticly.* Spelt "antiquely" in the early eds., which use *antique* and *antick* interchangeably without regard to the meaning. Cf. *Macb.* p. 234.

Show. The early eds. and many modern ones have "and show." Spedding suggested the emendation.

Outward hideousness = "what in *Hen. V.* iii. 6. 81 is called 'a *horrid suit* of the camp'" (Steevens).

97. *Off.* The early eds. have "of;" corrected by Theo. *Dangerous* = threatening.

101. *Wake.* Rouse, excite. Cf. *Rich. II.* i. 3. 132: "To wake our peace." See also *Rich. III.* i. 3. 288. Hanmer reads "rack" here, and Warb. "wrack." "Waste" has also been suggested.

104. *Full of proof.* Fully proved. Cf. "full of rest" in 1 *Hen. IV.* iv. 3. 27 and *J. C.* iv. 3. 202, etc.

113. *Almost a fray.* Rowe omitted *almost*, but, as Halliwell notes, the repetition is quite in Shakespeare's manner.

114. *Had like.* See *A. Y. L.* p. 197, note on *And like.* For *with* = by, see *Gr.* p. 193.

117. *I doubt.* I suspect. Cf. *M. W.* i. 4. 42: "I doubt he be not well," etc.

119. *In a false quarrel,* etc. Cf. 2 *Hen. VI.* iii. 2. 233: "Thrice is he arm'd that hath his quarrel just," etc.

122. *High-proof.* In a high degree; used by S. only here.

127. *As we do the minstrels.* "An allusion perhaps to the itinerant sword dancers" (Douce). Schmidt makes *draw* = draw the bow of a fiddle; Coll. (so D. and Halliwell) = draw the instruments from their cases.

ACT V. SCENE I.

128. *Pleasure.* Cf. *M. W.* i. 1. 251: "what I do is to pleasure you;" *M. of V.* i. 3. 7: "will you pleasure me?" etc.

131. *Care killed a cat.* A familiar old proverb. Cf. B. J., *Every Man in His Humour*, i. 3: "hang sorrow, care 'll kill a cat," etc.

133. *In the career*, etc. The metaphor is taken from the tilting-field, and is carried out by Claudio in his reply.

135. *Staff.* Lance. See *Macb.* pp. 250, 253. *Broke cross* broken crosswise, and not by a direct thrust. The former was considered disgraceful. See *A. Y. L.* p. 181, note on *Traverse.*

137. *By this light.* A common oath. Cf. *Temp.* ii. 2. 154, iii. 2. 17. *L. L.* iv. 3. 10, *K. John*, i. 1. 259, etc. See also v. 4. 92 below. So "by this good light" (*Temp.* ii. 2. 147, *W. T.* ii. 3. 182), "by this day and this light" (*Hen. V.* iv. 8. 66), "God's light!" (*2 Hen. IV.* ii. 4. 142, 159), etc.

139. *To turn his girdle.* "Large belts were worn with the buckle before, but for wrestling the buckle was turned behind, to give the adversary a fairer grasp at the girdle. To turn the buckle behind, therefore, was a challenge" (Holt White). Farmer cites a letter from Winwood's *Memorials*, in which Winwood, writing from Paris, in 1602, about an affront he received there from an Englishman, says: "I said what I spake was not to make him angry. He replied, if I were angry, I might turn the buckle of my girdle behind me." Cf. Cowley, *On the Government of Oliver Cromwell:* "The next month he swears by the living God, that he will turn them out of doors, and he does so in his princely way of threatening, bidding them turne the buckles of their girdles behind them." Halliwell explains the passage: "you may change your temper or humour, alter it to the opposite side;" W. and J. H. take it that the girdle is turned to get at the sword-hilt.

143. *How.* In whatever way. Cf. iii. 1. 60 above. *With what* with whatever weapon.

144. *Do me right.* Give me satisfaction; that is, accept my challenge. Cf. i. 1. 215 above, and see *A. Y. L.* p. 165. *Protest* = proclaim.

150. *Capon.* Perhaps, as Schmidt suggests, with a play on the word (= *cap on*, that is, a fool's cap, or coxcomb); as in *Cymb.* ii. 1. 25: "You are cock and capon too; and you crow, cock, with your comb on." Cf. *C. of E.* iii. 1. 32.

Curiously. Carefully, nicely. Cf. *T. of S.* iv. 3. 144: "The sleeves curiously cut."

151. *Naught.* Good for nothing. See *A. Y. L.* p. 142.

A woodcock. The bird was supposed to have no brains, and was therefore a popular metaphor for a fool. See *Ham.* pp. 191, 275.

157. *Just.* See on ii. 1. 24 above.

159. *A wise gentleman.* This seems to have been used ironically, as *wiseacre* is now.

He hath the tongues. That is, he knows foreign languages. Cf. *T. G. of V.* iv. 1. 33:

"*2 Outlaw.* Have you the tongues?
Valentine. My youthful travel therein made me happy."

163. *Trans-shape.* Caricature, "spell backward" (iii. 1. 61 above).

165. *Properest.* Handsomest. Cf. ii. 3. 166 above.

169. *Deadly.* Implacably. Adjectives are often used as adverbs (Gr. 1), especially those ending in *-ly.* Cf. *A. W.* v. 3. 117: "thou didst hate her deadly;" 3 *Hen. VI.* i. 4. 84: "I hate thee deadly;" *Cor.* ii. 1. 67: "they lie deadly," etc.

171. *God.* The Coll. MS. substitutes "who." There is an allusion to *Gen.* iii. 8.

173. *The savage bull's horns.* See i. 1. 231 fol.

190. *In his doublet and hose.* That is, without his cloak; perhaps, as Steevens suggests, because going to fight a duel. Cf. *M. W.* iii. 1. 46, where Page says to Evans, "In your doublet and hose this raw rheumatic day!" and Evans replies, "There is reasons and causes for it," referring to the duel he is about to fight. Boswell believes that "the words are probably meant to express what Rosalind in *A. Y. L.* [iii. 2. 400] terms the 'careless desolation' of a lover." Perhaps we need not see more in the passage than a hit at Benedick's being in such profound earnest, having laid aside his wit as he might his cloak.

193. *A doctor.* A learned man. For *to*=in comparison to, see *Ham.* p. 183.

194. *Soft you.* "Hold, stop" (Schmidt). See *M. N. D.* p. 176.

Let me be. The reading of both quarto and folio. Halliwell adopts Capell's suggestion of "let be," and quotes Palsgrave, 1530: "I let be, I let alone; let be this nyceenesse, my frende."

Pluck up, etc. "Rouse thyself, my heart, and be prepared for serious consequences!" (Steevens). Cf. *T. of S.* iv. 3. 38: "Pluck up thy spirits."

197. *Reasons.* Some see here a pun on *reasons* and *raisins,* as in 1 *Hen. IV.* ii. 4. 264: "if reasons were as plenty as blackberries." There is no doubt that *reasons* was pronounced like *raisins.* Cf. the pun on *meat* (pronounced *mate*) and *maid* in *T. G. of V.* i. 2. 68.

201. *Hearken after.* Inquire concerning. Cf. *Rich. III.* i. 1. 54: "He hearkens after prophecies and dreams" (Schmidt).

212. *Division.* Disposition, arrangement; as in *Oth.* i. 1. 23: "the division of a battle."

213. *Well suited.* "That is, one meaning is put into many different dresses; the Prince having asked the same question in four modes of speech" (Johnson). Cf. *Hen. V.* iv. 2. 53: "Description cannot suit itself in words," etc.

214. *Who.* Whom. Cf. i. 1. 187 above. Gr. 274.

215. *To your answer.* To answer for your conduct; that is, in a legal sense. Cf. *Hen. VIII.* iv. 2. 18:

"Arrested him at York, and brought him forward,
As a man sorely tainted, to his answer," etc.

216. *Cunning.* Knowing, wise. Cf. *T. of S.* ii. 1. 56: "Cunning in music and the mathematics," etc.

219. *Wisdoms.* See on iv. 1. 185 above, and cf. *Ham.* i. 2. 15: "Your better wisdoms," etc.

222. *Incensed.* Instigated. Cf. *W. T.* v. 1. 61:

"She had; and would incense me
To murder her I married."

See also *Rich. III.* iii. 1. 152, iii. 2. 29, etc. Nares takes the word in the present passage, and in *Rich. III.* to be properly *insense* (= to put sense into, instruct, inform), "a provincial expression still quite current in Staffordshire, and probably Warwickshire."
227. *Upon.* See on iv. 1. 221 above, and cf. 235 just below.
231. *Whiles.* See on iv. 1. 217 above.
233. *Practice.* Plotting. See on iv. 1. 186 above.
234. *Compos'd.* Wholly made up. Cf. *Temp.* iii. 1. 9:

"O, she is
Ten times more gentle than her father 's crabbed,
And he 's compos'd of harshness."

237. *That I lov'd it first.* That is, *in* which I loved it first. The preposition is often thus omitted in relative sentences. See Gr. 394.
248. *Art thou,* etc. The folio has "Art thou thou the slaue," and some modern eds. follow it in repeating *thou;* but this injures the metre and does not add to the sense. Even W. follows the quarto here.
255. *Bethink you of it.* Think of it, consider it. Cf. *T. N.* iii. 4. 327: " he hath better bethought him of his quarrel ;" *Rich. III.* ii. 2. 96:

"Madam, bethink you, like a careful mother,
Of the young prince your son," etc.

258. *Impose me to.* Impose on me; which is elsewhere the form of expression in S. Cf. *L. L. L.* iii. 1. 130: "impose on thee nothing but this," etc.
266. *Possess.* Inform. Cf. *M. of V.* i. 3. 65: "Is he yet possess'd How much ye would?"
268. *Labour.* For the transitive use, cf. *Rich. III.* i. 4. 253: "That he would labour my delivery," etc.
Invention. Imagination. Cf. *Hen. V.* prol. 2: "the brightest heaven of invention," etc.
269. *Hang her an epitaph,* etc. It was the custom of the time to affix memorial verses to the *herse* or canopy of black cloth erected temporarily over the tomb. Ben Jonson's well-known tribute to the Countess of Pembroke, "Underneath this sable hearse," etc., is said to have been written for such a purpose.
275. *And she alone,* etc. The poet seems to have forgotten that he has given Antonio a *son* in i. 2. 1 above. See on i. 1. 287 above.
282. *Naughty.* See on iv. 2. 66 above.
284. *Pack'd.* Implicated, a confederate. Cf. *C. of E.* v. 1. 219: "The goldsmith there, were he not pack'd with her," etc.
288. *By her.* About her. Cf. *M. of V.* i. 2. 60: "How say you by the French lord?" *L. L. L.* iv. 3. 150: "I would not have him know so much by me," etc. Gr. 145.
293. *A lock.* Cf. iii. 3. 153 above. Prynne, in 1628, wrote a treatise entitled "The Unlovelinesse of Love-lockes, or a discourse proving the wearing of a locke to be unseemly ;" and in his *Histriomastix* he speaks of "long, unshorne, love-provoking haire, and lovelockes growne now too much in fashion with comly pages, youthes, and lewd, effeminate, ruffianly persons."
Borrows money in God's name. That is, begs it; alluding

xix. 17 (Steevens). Halliwell says that this phrase was used in the counterfeit passports of the beggars, as appears from Dekker's *English Villanies*. He also cites Percivale's *Dictionarie in Spanish and English*, 1599: "*Pordioséros*, men that aske for God's sake, beggers."

294. *Hath used.* Hath used to do, has made a practice of. Cf. *J. C.* i. 1. 14: "a trade that I may use with a safe conscience," etc.

302. *God save the foundation!* "The customary phrase employed by those who received alms at the gates of religious houses" (Steevens).

316. *Lewd.* Vile, base. See *Rich. II.* p. 152. Cf. *Acts*, xvii. 5. Halliwell quotes Baret, *Alvearie:* "Lewd, ingratious, naughtie, *improbus, pravus, impurus.*"

SCENE II.—5. There is a play on *style* and *stile*, and on *come over* in the senses of *surpass* and *get over* (Schmidt). Cf. *L. L. L.* i. 1. 201: "Well, sir, be it as the style shall give us cause to climb in the merriness;" *Id.* iv. 1. 98:

"*Boyet.* I am much deceiv'd but I remember the style.
Princess. Else your memory is bad, going o'er it erewhile."

7. *Shall I always keep below stairs?* That is, in the servant's room, and never get married (Schmidt). Theo. wished to read "above stairs," and Steevens suggested "keep men below stairs."

14. *I give thee the bucklers.* I yield thee the victory. Steevens quotes Greene, *Coney-Catching*, 1592: "At this his master laught, and was glad, for further advantage, to yield the bucklers to his prentise;" and Holland's *Pliny:* "it goeth against his stomach to yeeld the gauntlet and give the bucklers."

19. *Pikes.* "The circular *bucklers* of the 16th century, now called more commonly *targets*, had frequently a central spike, or *pike*, usually affixed by a screw. It was probably found convenient to detach this spike occasionally; for instance, in cleaning the buckler, etc. *Vice* is the French *vis*, a screw" (Thoms).

24. *The God of love*, etc. The beginning of an old song by William Elderton (Ritson).

30. *Carpet-mongers.* Carpet knights, effeminate persons. Cf. *T. N.* iii. 4. 258: "He is knight, dubbed with unhatched rapier, and on carpet consideration."

34. *No rhyme to 'lady' but 'baby.'* This rhyme occurs in the *Musarum Deliciæ*, quoted by Halliwell:

"Whilst all those naked bedlams, painted babies,
Spottified faces, and Frenchified ladies."

37. *Festival terms.* In distinction from every-day language. Cf. *M. W.* iii. 2. 69: "he writes verses, he speaks holiday;" and 1 *Hen. IV.* i. 3. 46: "With many holiday and lady terms." See also *M. of V.* ii. 9. 98: "highday wit," etc.

42. *I came.* That is, came *for.* See on v. 1. 237 above.

45. *Words is.* See Gr. 333.

48. *His.* Its. See Gr. 228.

50. *Undergoes.* Is subject to.

Subscribe him. Write him down, proclaim him.

67. *Of good neighbours.* "That is, when men were not envious, but every one gave another his due" (Warb.).

69. *Monument.* The folio has "monuments" and "bells ring."

71. *Question.* That's the question. Some eds. print "Question?" do you ask the question?

72. *Rheum.* Tears. Cf. *K. John*, iii. 1. 22: "Why holds thine eye that lamentable rheum?" (see also iv. 1. 33 and iv. 3. 108); *Cor.* v. 6. 46: "a few drops of women's rheum;" *Ham.*, ii. 2. 529: "with bisson rheum," etc.

73. *Don Worm.* Conscience was formerly represented under the symbol of a worm. Cf. *Rich. III.* i. 3. 222: "The worm of conscience still begnaw thy soul!" In an account of the expenses connected with one of the old Coventry mysteries, we find "Item, payd to ij wormes of conscience, xvj. d."

83. *Yonder's old coil.* In modern slang, "there's a high old time." For *old* as a "colloquial intensive," cf. *M. of V.* iv. 2. 15: "old swearing;" *Macb.* ii. 3. 2: "old turning of the key," etc. See *Macb.* p. 197. *Coil*=turmoil, confusion. Halliwell cites Cotgrave, *Fr. Dict.*: "*Faire le diable de vauuert,* to play reaks, to keep an old coile, a horrible stirre." See also on iii. 3. 85 above.

84. *Abused.* Deceived. Cf. *Temp.* v. 1. 112: "Or some enchanted trifle to abuse me," etc. See also *Macb.* p. 187.

87. *Presently.* Immediately. See on i. 1. 74 above.

SCENE III.—3. *Done to death.* A common phrase in old writers. Cf. *Promos and Cassandra*, 1578: "Is my Andrugio done to death?" Marlowe, *Lust's Dominion:* "Thinking her own son is done to death;" Chapman, *Homer:* "Hector (in Chi) to death is done," etc. See also 2 *Hen. VI.* iii. 2. 179: "Why, Warwick, who should do the duke to death?"

5. *Guerdon.* Recompense. Cf. *L. L. L.* iii. 1. 170: "There's thy guerdon." S. uses the noun only twice; but he has the verb in 2 *Hen. VI.* i. 4. 49 and 3 *Hen. VI.* iii. 3. 191.

10. *Dumb.* The folio reading; the quarto misprints "dead."

11. *Music.* Musicians; as often. Cf. *L. L. L.* v. 2. 211: "Play, music, then!" *M. of V.* v. 1. 98: "It is your music, madam, of the house;" *Hen. VIII.* iv. 2. 94: "Bid the music leave; they are harsh to me," etc.

13. *Knight.* The Coll. MS. substitutes "bright;" but cf. *A. W.* i. 3. 120: "Dian no queen of virgins, that would suffer her poor knight surprised, without rescue in the first assault or ransom afterward." Malone quotes *Two Noble Kinsmen:*

> "O sacred, shadowy, cold, and constant queen,
> ... who to thy female knights
> Allow'st no more blood than will make a blush,
> Which is their order's robe," etc.

For the rhyme of *night* and *knight*, cf. *M. W.* ii. 1. 15, 16.

21. *Heavily, heavily.* The quarto reading; the folio has "*Heauen'y, heauenly,*" which is adopted by K., St., and W. "Uttered heavenly" is

explained as = "expelled (outer-ed) by the power of Heaven." Walker calls the folio reading "a most absurd error, generated (*ut sæpe*) by the corruption of an uncommon word into a common one." In *Ham.* ii. 2. 300. the folio has the same misprint of *heavenly* for *heavily*. Halliwell explains the passage thus: "The slayers of the virgin knight are performing a solemn requiem on the body of Hero, and they invoke Midnight and the shades of the dead to assist, until *her* death be *uttered*, that is, proclaimed, published, sorrowfully, sorrowfully." Schmidt says: "the cry, *Graves, yawn and yield your dead*, shall be raised till death, etc.;" we prefer, with Halliwell and Walker, to consider these words as "a call upon the surrounding dead to come forth from their graves, as auditors or sharers in the solemn lamentation." J. H. reads "heavenly," and takes the meaning to be, "Let these words be uttered in a heavenly spirit until death, that is, so long as I live!"

22. *Now, unto*, etc. Both quarto and folio assign this speech to "*Lo*." (*Lord*), but Rowe restored it to Claudio, to whom it clearly belongs.

25. *Wolves.* Associated with night, as in *M. N. D.* v. 1. 379, *Macb.* ii. 1. 53, etc. The lines that follow are one of the most exquisite of Shakespeare's word-pictures of the sunrise. Cf. Milton's "dappled dawn" in *L'Allegro*.

29. *Several.* Separate. See *Temp.* p. 131. Cf. its use as a noun (=individual) in *W. T.* i. 2. 226, and see also *Hen. V.* p. 146.

30. *Weeds.* Garments, dress. Cf. *M. N. D.* ii. 1. 256: "Weed wide enough to wrap a fairy in;" *Id.* ii. 2. 71: "Weeds of Athens he doth wear," etc.

32. *Speed 's.* That is, speed us (3d person, imperative); Thirlby's emendation of the "speeds" of the early eds. "Claudio could not know, without being a prophet, that this new proposed match should have any luckier event than that designed with Hero; certainly, therefore, this should be a wish." Malone objects to the contraction *speed 's;* but D. compares *L. L. L.* ii. 1. 25: "Therefore to 's seemeth it a needful course." An example more in point would be *W. T.* i. 2. 91: "I prithee tell me; cram 's with praise, and make 's," etc. See also *Id.* i. 2. 94: "you may ride 's;" *A. and C.* ii. 7. 134: "give 's your hand," etc.

33. *Render up this woe.* Offer this woful tribute. Cf. *T. A.* i. 1. 160:

"Lo! at this tomb my tributary tears
I render for my brethren's obsequies;"

and *K. John*, v. 7. 110: "O, let us pay the time but needful woe!"

SCENE IV.—3. *Upon.* On account of. See on iv. 1. 221 above.

6. *Question.* Inquiry, investigation.

7. *Sort.* Turn out. Cf. iv. 1. 238 above.

8. *By faith enforc'd.* Compelled by my pledge, obliged in honour. Cf. *T. G. of V.* i. 2. 63: "inward joy enforc'd my heart to smile," etc.

17. *Confirm'd countenance.* Steady face. Cf. *Cor.* i. 3. 65: "has such a confirmed countenance."

28. *For.* As for. Cf. iii. 2. 85 above.

30. *State.* The reading of the early eds. changed by Johnson to "es-

tate." Steevens makes *marriage* a trisyllable; as in *M. of V.* ii. 9. 13, *T. of S.* iii. 2. 142, *R. of L.* 221, etc.
33. *Comes.* See Gr. 336.
34. *Assembly.* A quadrisyllable here. Cf. *Cor.* i. 1. 159: "You, the great toe of this assembly." Gr. 477.
37. *To marry with.* Cf. *M. N. D.* i. 1. 40: "to marry with Demetrius," etc.
38. *Ethiope.* See *M. N. D.* p. 166.
43. *Bull.* See on v. 1. 173 above.
45. *Europa.* Europe; with an obvious play upon the word. For the allusion, cf. *M. W.* v. 5. 4 and *T. of S.* i. 1. 173.
52. *Comes.* Changed by Rowe to "come." Gr. 335.
59. *Like of me.* Cf. *P. P.* 212:

"It was a lordling's daughter, the fairest one of three,
That liked of her master as well as well might be;"

A. W. ii. 3. 131:

"thou dislikest
Of virtue for the name," etc.

See Gr. 177.
62. *Certainer.* See Gr. 7.
63. *Defil'd.* The quarto reading; the folio omits the word. The Coll. MS. has "belied," which Coll. defends on the ground that Hero would not be likely to speak of herself as *defiled.* Of course Hero meant defiled by slander (cf. what Leonato says immediately after), and now that her innocence was established no one present could misunderstand her.
66. *Whiles.* See on iv. 1. 217 above.
67. *Qualify.* Moderate, abate. Cf. *Lear*, i. 2. 176: "till some little time hath qualified the heat of his displeasure," etc.
68. *After that.* For *that* as a "conjunctional affix," see Gr. 287.
69. *Largely.* "At large" (*M. N. D.* v. 1. 152, etc.), in detail.
70. *Familiar.* A quadrisyllable. Gr. 479.
71. *Presently.* See on i. 1. 74 above.
72. *Soft and fair.* A common phrase of the time. Cf. *soft you*, v. 1. 194 above.
82. *No such matter.* See on ii. 3. 198 above.
89. *Writ.* Used often by S. both as past tense and participle; but we have *written* just above. Gr. 343.
90. *Affection unto.* Love for. Cf. *Lear*, i. 2. 94: "my affection to your honour," etc.
92. *By this light.* See on v. 1. 137 above. Cf. *by this good day* just below.
97. *Peace*, etc. Given by the early eds. to *Leonato;* corrected by Theo., who added the stage-direction. Cf. *Rich. II.* v. 1. 95: "One kiss shall stop our mouths," etc. See also ii. 1. 278 above.
100. *Flout.* Mock, jeer. See on i. 1. 162 above.
102. *Beaten with brains.* That is, mocked. Schmidt compares *Ham.* ii. 2. 376: "much throwing about of brains" (= much satirical controversy).

108. *In that.* Inasmuch as. Cf. *A. Y. L.* i. 1. 50: "in that you are the first-born," etc.

112. *Double-dealer.* "One notoriously unfaithful in love or wedlock" (St.).

113. *Exceeding.* For the adverbial use, see on ii. 3. 146 above, and cf. iii. 4. 22, 47, etc.

119. *Of my word.* Upon my word. Cf. *R. and J.* i. 1. 1, etc. Gr. 169.

121. *More reverend.* That is, because it is used by elderly people. The tipped staff was one of the usual accompaniments of old age (Halliwell). Cf. Chaucer, *C. T.* 7322: "His felaw [one of the begging friars] had a staf typped with horn." In *horn* there is the well-worn hit at the cuckold.

124. *With.* By; as in ii. 1. 53, iii. 1. 66, 79, and v. 1. 115 above. Gr. 193.

126. *Brave.* Becoming, fitting (Schmidt); or perhaps with a touch of irony, as often. Cf. *Temp.* iii. 2. 12, *A. Y. L.* iii. 4. 43, *Ham.* ii. 2. 611, etc.

ADDENDUM.

Note on p. 23.—To the comments of Verplanck, Furnivall, and Gervinus on Campbell's opinion of Beatrice, may be added the following from Charles Cowden Clarke's *Shakespeare-Characters*, p. 295:

"In the general estimation of the world, Beatrice is one of those who wear their characters inside out. They have no reserves with society, for they require none. They may, perhaps, presume upon, or rather forget that they possess a mercurial temperament, which, when unreined, is apt to start from its course and inconvenience their fellow-travellers; but such a propensity is not an 'odious' one—it is not hateful; and this is the only feature in the character of Beatrice that Mr. Campbell could object to. She is warm-hearted, generous; has a noble contempt of baseness of every kind; is wholly untinctured with jealousy; is the first to break out into invective when her cousin Hero is treated in that scoundrel manner by her affianced husband at the very altar, and even makes it a *sine qua non* with Benedick to prove his love for herself by challenging the traducer of her cousin. . . .

"Beatrice is not without consciousness of her power of wit; but it is rather the delight she takes in something that is an effluence of her own glad nature, than for any pride of display. She enjoys its exercise, too, as a means of playful despotism over one whom she secretly admires, while openly tormenting. . . .

"The fact is, like many high-spirited women, Beatrice possesses a fund of hidden tenderness beneath her exterior gayety and sarcasm—none the less profound from being withheld from casual view, and very seldom allowed to bewray itself. As proof of this, witness her affection for her uncle Leonato, and his strong esteem and love for her; her passionate attachment to her cousin Hero, and the occasional but extremely significant betrayals of her partiality for Benedick; her very seeking out opportunities to torment him being one proof (especially in a woman of her disposition and breeding) of her preference; for women do not banter a man they dislike—they mentally send him to Coventry, and do not raise him into importance by offering an objection, still less a repartee or a sarcasm. The only time we see Beatrice alone, and giving utterance to the thoughts of her heart—that is, in soliloquy, which is the dramatic medium of representing self-communion [iii. 1. 107-116]—her words are full of warm and feminine tenderness,—words that probably would not seem so pregnant of love-import, coming from another woman, more prone to express such feeling; but, from Beatrice, meaning much. It is the very transcript of an honest and candid heart. . . .

"It is not unusual to designate her (as well as Portia) as a 'masculine woman.' I can only say that every man who expresses this opinion commits a piece of egoism, for both women are endowed with qualities, moral and intellectual, that any man might be proud to inherit. And here it is impossible to forego a passing remark upon the generous, indeed the chivalrous conduct of Shakespeare in portraying his women. Of all the writers that ever existed, no one ought to stand so high in the love and gratitude of women as he. He has indeed been their champion, their laureate, their brother, their friend. He has been the man to lift them from a state of vassalage and degradation, wherein they were the mere toys, when not the she-serfs, of a sensual tyranny; and he has asserted their prerogative, as intellectual creatures, to be the companions (in the best sense), the advisers, the friends, the equals of men. He has endowed them with the true spirit of Christianity and brotherly love, 'enduring all things, forgiving all things, hoping all things;' and it is no less remarkable that, with a prodigality of generosity, he has not unfrequently placed the heroes in his stories at a disadvantage with them. Observe, for instance, the two characters of Hero and Claudio in this very play." . . .

THE "TIME-ANALYSIS" OF THE PLAY.—This is summed up by Mr. P. A. Daniel (*Trans. of New Shaks. Soc.* 1877-79, p. 144) as follows:

"In the endeavour to make the action of the play agree as far as possible with Leonato's determination in Act II. sc. i., that the marriage of Claudio and Hero shall take place on 'Monday . . . which is hence a just seven-night,' I have supposed the following days to be represented on the stage:
1. Monday. Act I. and sc. i. of Act II.
2. Tuesday. Act II. sc. ii.
3. Wednesday. Act II. sc. iii.*
    Thursday. ⎫
    Friday.   ⎬ Blank.
    Saturday. ⎭

---

* "I place this scene in the third day (Wednesday). The love conspirators would scarcely defer their attempt on Benedick's peace of mind to a later date; but yet, for the verisimilitude of their description of Beatrice's passion 'she'll be up twenty times a night, and there will she sit in her smock till she have writ a sheet of paper,' etc.—we must suppose a night or two to have passed since the opening scene."

4. Sunday. Act III. sc. i.–iii.*
5. Monday. Act III. sc. iv. and v., Act IV. sc. i. and ii., Act V. sc. i., ii., and part of iii.
6. Tuesday. Act V. sc. iii. (in part) and sc. iv.

The first Tuesday even in this scheme might very well be left a blank, and the sc. ii. of Act II. be included in the opening Monday.

I believe, however, that just as the Prince forgets his determination to stay 'at the least a month' at Messina, so the 'just seven-night' to the wedding was also either forgotten or intentionally set aside, and that only four *consecutive* days are actually included in the action of the drama.

1. Act I. and Act II., sc. i. and ii.
2. Act II. sc. iii. and Act III. sc. i.–iii.
3. Act III. sc. iv. and v., Act IV., Act V. sc. i., ii., and part of iii.
4. Act V. part of sc. iii. and sc. iv."

---

* "Note. in the opening speech of scene ii. Don Pedro says, 'I do but stay till your marriage be consummate, and then go I toward Arragon.' He has changed his mind, then, since the opening day, when he proposed to stay '*at the least a month,*' with Leonato."

INDEX OF WORDS AND PHRASES EXPLAINED.

a (with verbal), 145.
abused (=deceived), 169.
account, to make an, 129.
ache (pronunciation), 150.
achiever, 118.
Adam, 124.
advertisement, 162.
advise, 158.
afeard, 138.
affect (=love), 124.
affection, 135.
affection unto, 171.
after (adverb), 125.
agate, 141.
aim at, 144.
alms, 138.
ancientry, 129.
angel (play upon), 136.
answer (legal), 166.
antic (=buffoon), 141.
anticly, 164.
apparitions (pronunciation), 155.
apprehension, 150.
approved (=proved), 134, 153, 158.
argument (=discourse), 142.
argument (=proof), 139.
argument (=subject), 123, 135.
arras, 128.
as (omitted), 138.
as full as (=fully as), 140.
assembly (quadrisyllable), 171.
at a word, 130.
Ate, 132.
attired in wonder, 155.

badge, 118.
baldrick, 123.
barns (play upon), 150.
bear-herd, 129
bear in hand, 158.
bear it coldly, 145.
beaten with brains, 171.
become of (=come of), 157.
being that, 158.

bent, 139, 156.
beshrew, 152.
bethink you, 167.
bill (play upon), 148.
bills, setting up, 118.
bills (weapons), 145.
bird-bolt, 119.
biting, 156.
black (=dark), 141.
blazon, 133.
block, 130.
blood (=disposition), 127.
blood (=passion), 131, 138.
bloods, 147.
boarded, 130.
Borachio (derivation), 147.
borrow money in God's name, 167.
both in a tale, 160.
brave, 172.
break with, 125.
breathing (=interval), 134.
bring (=accompany), 143.
broke cross, 165.
bucklers, to give the, 168.
by (=about), 167.
by (=from), 155.
by the mass, 160.
by this of time, 117.
by this light, 165.

candle-wasters, 161.
canker (=canker-rose), 127.
capon (play upon), 165.
Cardinis benedictus, 150.
care killed a cat, 165.
carpet-mongers, 168.
carriage (=bearing), 127.
carry (=manage), 139, 157.
censured (=judged), 139.
certainer, 171.
chain (usurer's), 131.
Cham, the great, 132.
charge (=burden), 127.
charge (constable's), 145.
cheapen, 136.
cheer, 128.
chid at, 155.

cinque-pace, 129.
circumstances, 145.
civil (play upon), 133.
claw flatter, 126.
clerk, 130.
cog, 164.
coil, 146, 169.
commendable (accent), 141.
commodity (play upon), 148.
composed, 167.
conceit, 133.
conditions, 144.
conference, 139, 140.
confirmed countenance, 170.
conjectures suspicion, 154.
consummate, 142.
contemptible, 131.
content your e.t., 164.
controlment, 127.
convert (intransitive), 121.
conveyance, 132.
counsel, 139.
Count Comfect, 152.
county (=count), 133, 134, 150.
courtesies, 159.
cousins, 126.
cry you mercy, 126.
cunning (=knowing), 166.
curiously, 165.
curtsy, 129, 159.
cuts, 149.

daffed, 138, 163.
dangerous, 164.
deadly (adverb), 166.
dear, 121.
defeat (=ruin), 153.
defend (=forbid), 129, 160.
deny (=refuse), 158.
deprave (=slander), 164.
difference, for a, 120.
discover (=reveal), 126, 138, 144.
displeasure to, 135.
division, 141.
do him so ill-well, 130.
do me right, 168.

176 INDEX OF WORDS AND PHRASES EXPLAINED.

doctor (= learned man), 166.
Dogberry, 145.
Don Worm, 169.
done to death, 169.
dotage, 138.
double-dealer, 172.
doubt (= suspect), 164
down sleeves, 149.
draw, 164
draw (play upon), 143.
dumb show, 139.
dumps, 137.

eat (= eaten), 156.
eat your word, 158
ecstasy (= madness), 138.
eftest, 160
enamoured on, 131.
encounters, 154.
enforced (= compelled), 170.
engaged (= pledged), 153
enraged (= intense), 138.
entertained for, 127
estimation (= worth), 133.
Ethiope, 171.
Europa, 171.
even (= plain), 158.
every day, to-morrow, 142.
exceeding (adverb), 138, 172.
exceeds (intransitive), 148.
excellent (adverb), 138.
eye and prospect, 157.

faith, 120, 170.
familiar (quadrisyllable), 171.
fancy (= love), 143
fashion-monging, 164.
father (verb), 121.
favour (= face), 129.
fence, 163.
festival terms, 168.
fetch in, 123.
fine (= end), 123.
fire in the ears, 142.
fleet, 162.
flight (= arrow), 119.
flout (= mock), 164, 171.
flout old ends, 124.
flouting Jack, 121.
foining, 163.
fool, 133.
for (= as for), 144, 170.
fore, 139
frame (= devising), 156.
frame (= order), 155.
framed (= devised), 163.
from (= away from), 141.
full of proof, 164.
furnish (= dress), 142.

gallop, false, 151.
girdle, to turn his, 165.
gives me out, 131.

go about (= undertake), 126, 154, 160.
go in (= join in), 122.
go to church, 134.
go to the world, 133.
God save the foundation! 168.
God's a good man, 152.
good den, 144, 162.
good year, the, 126.
grace (= favour), 127, 135.
gracious (= lovely), 154.
guarded (= trimmed), 124.
guerdon, 169.
guts, 137.

had as lief, 137.
had like, 164.
haggards, 140.
hale (= draw), 137.
halfpence, 138.
hand, a dry, 130.
hang (play upon), 143.
hangman, 143.
happiness, outward, 139.
have it full, 121.
hear tell, 134.
heart-burned, 128.
heavily, 169.
Hercules, the shaven, 147.
high-proof, 164.
his (= its), 168.
hobby-horses, 144.
hold friends with, 121.
hold it up, 138.
holds you well, 144.
holp, 119.
honest as the skin between his brows, 151.
how (= however), 141, 165.
Hundred Merry Tales, 130.

I'll none, 129, 135.
idea (= image), 157.
important (= importunate), 129.
impose me to, 167.
impossible, 130, 132.
in (= into), 135.
in dearness of heart, 145.
in question, 148.
in respect of, 149.
in such a kind, 156.
in that, 172.
in the fleet, 130.
in the height, 158.
incensed, 166.
infinite, 138.
instances, 135.
intend (= pretend), 135.
invention, 156, 167.
inwardness, 158.

Jacks, 164.
jade's trick, 121.
Jew (contemptuous), 140.
just (= exact), 134.
just (= just so), 129, 165.

keep below stairs, 168.
kid-fox, 136.
kind (= natural), 118.
kindly (= natural), 154
kindness (= tenderness), 118.
knight (feminine), 169.

labour (transitive), 167.
lantern, 145.
lapwing, 140.
large (= free, broad), 139, 153.
largely, 171.
learn (= teach), 153.
leavy, 137.
let it cool, 139.
level (= aim), 158.
lewd (= vile), 168.
liberal (= licentious), 154.
light (play upon), 149.
Light o' love, 150.
like of me, 171.
limed, 142.
liver, 157.
lock (= love-lock), 148, 167.
lodge in a warren, a, 131.
low (of stature), 141.
lustihood, 163.
lute-string, 144.
luxurious (= lustful), 153.

mannerly (adverb), 129.
March-chick, 127.
marry with, 171.
match (= marry), 129.
matter (= sense), 134
may (= can), 135, 154, 158.
me, 128, 148.
measure (play upon), 129.
medicinable, 135.
meet with (= even with), 119.
merely (= entirely), 139.
mile (plural), 135.
mired, 155
misgovernment, 154.
misprising, 141.
misprision, 156.
misuse (= deceive), 135.
misused (= abused), 132.
model, 127.
moe, 137.
Montano, 118.
moral, 151, 162.
mortal, we are all, 120.
mortifying, 126.
mountain of affection, 134.
move (a question), 154.
music (= musicians), 169.

naught, 165.
naughty, 160, 167.
near (=intimate with), 130.
news (number), 125, 131.
night-gown, 149.
night-raven, 137.
no such matter, 122, 139, 171.
noble (play upon), 136.
non-come, 152.
not (transposed), 156.
note (=mark), 144.
nothing (pronunciation), 136.
nuptial, 154.

of (=by), 121.
of my word, 172.
off the matter, 151.
old, 169.
on (=of), 155.
only (transposed), 130, 143.
orchard (=garden), 126, 135.
orthography, 135.
ostentation, 157.
outfacing, 164.
outward hideousness, 164.
overborne, 138.
overmastered, 129.

packed, 167.
palabras, 151.
partridge wing, 130.
passion (=sorrow), 162.
patience (trisyllable), 161.
pent-house, 146.
Philemon's roof, 130.
piece of flesh, 161.
Pigmies, 133.
pikes, 168.
pleached, 140.
pleasant, 118.
please it, 121.
pleasure (verb), 165.
pluck up, 166.
possessed (=influenced), 148.
possessed (=informed), 167.
pound (plural), 121, 151.
practice (=plotting), 156, 167.
preceptial medicine, 162.
predestinate, 121.
present (=represent), 146.
presently, 121, 125, 135, 158, 169, 171.
press to death, 141.
Prester John, 132.
prized (=estimated), 142.
project, 141.
proof (=experience), 131.
proof (=trial), 153.
proper (=handsome), 139, 165.
proper (ironical), 127, 159.
propose (noun), 140.

proposing (conversing), 140.
protest (proclaim), 165.
push, 162.

quaint, 149.
qualify, 171.
quarrel to, a, 132.
queasy, 134.
question, 169.
quips, 139.
quit (- requite), 156.

rabato, 148.
rack, 157.
ready (=dressed), 150.
rearward, 154.
reasons (play upon), 166.
recheat, 123.
reclusive, 158.
reechy, 147.
remorse (=pity), 157.
render (give , 153.
render up this woe, 170.
reportingly, 142.
reprove (disprove), 139.
reverence, 162.
rheum (= tears), 169.
rob from, 127.

's (=it's), 148.
sad (=serious), 121, 134.
sadly (=seriously), 139.
salved, 125.
Saturn, born under, 126.
saving your reverence, 149.
scab (play upon), 146.
scambling, 164.
scape, 121.
scorn with my heels, 150.
season, 155.
self-endeared, 141.
sentences, 139
several (=separate), 170.
shames, 155.
shrewd, 128.
side sleeves, 149.
sigh away Sundays, 122.
simpleness, 141.
sits the wind, etc., 138.
slops, 143.
smirched, 147.
so (=provided that), 129.
soft and fair, 171.
soft you, 166.
sort (=fall out), 158, 170.
sort (=rank), 118.
speed 's, 170.
spell backward, 141.
spirits (monosyllable), 154.
squarer, 121.
staff (=lance), 165.
stale (=wanton), 135, 154.

stalk (verb), 137.
start-up, 128
still (constantly), 128.
stomach, 126.
stops of lute, 144
strain (family , 134.
strain (feeling , 161.
study, 157.
stuff, 140.
stuffed, 119.
style (play upon), 168.
style of gods, 162
subscribe, 168.
success (issue, 158.
sufferance, 162.
suffigance, 152.
suit (agree), 161.
sun-burnt, 133.
sure, 128.
swift (ready), 142.
sworn brother, 120.

take up (play upon), 148.
tax (= reproach , 119.
temper (mix), 135.
temporize, 124.
terminations, 132.
that, 125, 138, 171.
thee (them), 140, 153.
there 's an end, 130.
thick-pleached, 126.
this seven year, 147.
throughly, 157.
thy much, 154.
tickling (trisyllable), 142.
tire (- head-dress), 148.
't is once, 125.
to (in comparisons), 166.
to thy head, 162.
tongues, he hath the, 165.
toothache, charm for, 144.
toothpicker, 132.
trace (=walk), 140.
trans-shape, 165.
trencher-man, 119.
trial of a man, 163.
trim (ironical), 159.
trow, 150.
tuition, 124.
turned Turk, 150.
tyrant, 121.

unconfirmed, 147.
underborne, 149.
undergoes, 168.
untowardly, 145.
up and down, 130.
upon, 157, 160, 167, 170.
use (=interest), 133.
used (=practised), 168.

valuing of, 155.
Verges, 145.

178 INDEX OF WORDS AND PHRASES EXPLAINED.

vice (=screw), 168.
victual, 119.
vouchsafe, 143.

wag (=begone), 161.
wake (=rouse), 164.
weak, 141.
weeds (=dress), 170.
well-favoured, 145.
well-suited, 166.
what (=who), 118, 130.
what is he for a fool? 127.
when all's done, 137.

whiles, 157, 167, 171.
whisper (transitive), 140.
who (=whom), 122, 166.
willow (emblem of unhappy love), 131.
win me and wear me, 163.
winded, 123.
wisdoms, 166.
wish (=bid), 140.
wit (=wisdom), 139.
with (=by), 129, 172.
withal, 126, 140.
wits, five, 120.

woe, 170.
wolves, 170.
woo, 136.
woodcock (applied to a fool), 165.
woollen, in the, 129.
world to see, a, 151.
worm (causing toothache), 143.
worm (of conscience), 169.
would, 138.
wring (=writhe), 162.
writ (=written), 138, 171.

OMPHALE AND HERCULES (iii. 3. 124).

SHAKESPEARE.

WITH NOTES BY WM. J. ROLFE, Litt.D.

The Merchant of Venice.
The Tempest.
Julius Cæsar.
Hamlet.
As You Like It.
Henry the Fifth.
Macbeth.
Henry the Eighth.
A Midsummer-Night's Dream.
Richard the Second.
Richard the Third.
Much Ado About Nothing.
Antony and Cleopatra.
Romeo and Juliet.
Othello.
Twelfth Night.
The Winter's Tale.
King John.
Henry IV. Part I.
Henry IV. Part II.

King Lear.
The Taming of the Shrew.
All's Well That Ends Well.
Coriolanus.
Comedy of Errors.
Cymbeline.
Merry Wives of Windsor.
Measure for Measure.
Two Gentlemen of Verona.
Love's Labor 's Lost.
Timon of Athens.
Henry VI. Part I.
Henry VI. Part II.
Henry VI. Part III.
Troilus and Cressida.
Pericles, Prince of Tyre.
The Two Noble Kinsmen.
Poems.
Sonnets.
Titus Andronicus.

Illustrated. 16mo, Cloth, 56 cents per vol.; Paper, 40 cents per vol.
FRIENDLY EDITION, complete in 20 vols., 16mo, Cloth, $30 00; Half Calf, $60 00. (*Sold only in Sets.*)

In the preparation of this edition of the English Classics it has been the aim to adapt them for school and home reading, in essentially the same way as Greek and Latin Classics are edited for educational purposes. The chief requisites are a pure text (expurgated, if necessary), and the notes needed for its thorough explanation and illustration.

Each of Shakespeare's plays is complete in one volume, and is preceded by an Introduction containing the "History of the Play," the "Sources of the Plot," and "Critical Comments on the Play."

From HORACE HOWARD FURNESS, Ph.D., LL.D., *Editor of the "New Variorum Shakespeare."*

No one can examine these volumes and fail to be impressed with the conscientious accuracy and scholarly completeness with which they are edited. The educational purposes for which the notes are written Mr. Rolfe never loses sight of, but like "a well experienced archer hits the mark his eye doth level at."

From F. J. FURNIVALL, *Director of the New Shakspere Society, London.*

The merit I see in Mr. Rolfe's school editions of Shakspere's Plays over those most widely used in England is that Mr. Rolfe edits the plays as works of a poet, and not only as productions in Tudor English. Some editors think that all they have to do with a play is to state its source and explain its hard words and allusions ; they treat it as they would a charter or a catalogue of household furniture, and then rest satisfied. But Mr. Rolfe, while clearing up all verbal difficulties as carefully as any Dryasdust, always adds the choicest extracts he can find, on the spirit and special "note" of each play, and on the leading characteristics of its chief personages. He does *not* leave the student without help in getting at Shakspere's chief attributes, his characterization and poetic power. And every practical teacher knows that while every boy can look out hard words in a lexicon for himself, not one in a score can, unhelped, catch points of and realize character, and feel and express the distinctive individuality of each play as a poetic creation.

From Prof. EDWARD DOWDEN, LL.D., *of the University of Dublin, Author of "Shakspere: His Mind and Art."*

I incline to think that no edition is likely to be so useful for school and home reading as yours. Your notes contain so much accurate instruction, with so little that is superfluous ; you do not neglect the æsthetic study of the plays; and in externals, paper, type, binding, etc., you make a book "pleasant to the eye" (as well as "to be desired to make one wise")—no small matter, I think, with young readers and with old.

From EDWIN A. ABBOTT, M.A., *Author of "Shakespearian Grammar."*

I have not seen any edition that compresses so much necessary information into so small a space, nor any that so completely avoids the common faults of commentaries on Shakespeare—needless repetition, superfluous explanation, and unscholar-like ignoring of difficulties.

From HIRAM CORSON, M.A., *Professor of Anglo-Saxon and English Literature, Cornell University, Ithaca, N. Y.*

In the way of annotated editions of separate plays of Shakespeare for educational purposes, I know of none quite up to Rolfe's.

From Prof. F. J. CHILD, *of Harvard University.*

I read your "Merchant of Venice" with my class, and found it in every respect an excellent edition. I do not agree with my friend White in the opinion that Shakespeare requires but few notes—that is, if he is to be thoroughly understood. Doubtless he may be enjoyed, and many a hard place slid over. Your notes give all the help a young student requires, and yet the reader for pleasure will easily get at just what he wants. You have indeed been conscientiously concise.

Under date of July 25, 1879, Prof. CHILD *adds:* Mr. Rolfe's editions of plays of Shakespeare are very valuable and convenient books, whether for a college class or for private study. I have used them with my students, and I welcome every addition that is made to the series. They show care, research, and good judgment, and are fully up to the time in scholarship. I fully agree with the opinion that experienced teachers have expressed of the excellence of these books.

From Rev. A. P. PEABODY, D.D., *Professor in Harvard University.*

I regard your own work as of the highest merit, while you have turned the labors of others to the best possible account. I want to have the higher classes of our schools introduced to Shakespeare chief of all, and then to other standard English authors; but this cannot be done to advantage unless under a teacher of equally rare gifts and abundant leisure, or through editions specially prepared for such use. I trust that you will have the requisite encouragement to proceed with a work so happily begun.

From the Examiner and Chronicle, N. Y.

We repeat what we have often said, that there is no edition of Shakespeare which seems to us preferable to Mr. Rolfe's. As mere specimens of the printer's and binder's art they are unexcelled, and their other merits are equally high. Mr. Rolfe, having learned by the practical experience of the class-room what aid the average student really needs in order to read Shakespeare intelligently, has put just that amount of aid into his notes, and no more. Having said what needs to be said, he stops there. It is a rare virtue in the editor of a classic, and we are proportionately grateful for it.

From the N. Y. Times.

This work has been done so well that it could hardly have been done better. It shows throughout knowledge, taste, discriminating judgment, and, what is rarer and of yet higher value, a sympathetic appreciation of the poet's moods and purposes.

From the Pacific School Journal, San Francisco.

This edition of Shakespeare's plays bids fair to be the most valuable aid to the study of English literature yet published. For educational purposes it is beyond praise. Each of the plays is printed in large clear type and on excellent paper. Every difficulty of the text is clearly explained by copious notes. It is remarkable how many new beauties one may discern in Shakespeare with the aid of the glossaries attached to these books. . . . Teachers can do no higher, better work than to inculcate a love for the best literature, and such books as these will best aid them in cultivating a pure and refined taste.

From the Christian Union, N. Y.

Mr. W J. Rolfe's capital edition of Shakespeare . . . by far the best edition for school and parlor use. We speak after some practical use of it in a village Shakespeare Club. The notes are brief but useful; and the necessary expurgations are managed with discriminating skill.

From the Academy, London.

Mr. Rolfe's excellent series of school editions of the Plays of Shakespeare. . . . They differ from some of the English ones in looking on the plays as something more than word-puzzles. They give the student helps and hints on the characters and meanings of the plays, while the word-notes are also full and posted up to the latest date. . . . Mr. Rolfe also adds to each of his books a most useful "Index of Words and Phrases Explained."

PUBLISHED BY HARPER & BROTHERS, NEW YORK.

☞ *The above works are for sale by all booksellers, or they will be sent by* HARPER *&* BROTHERS *to any address on receipt of price as quoted. If ordered sent by mail, 10 per cent. should be added to the price to cover cost of postage.*

OLIVER GOLDSMITH.

SELECT POEMS OF OLIVER GOLDSMITH. Edited, with Notes, by WILLIAM J. ROLFE, A.M., formerly Head Master of the High School, Cambridge, Mass. Illustrated. 16mo, Paper, 40 cents; Cloth, 56 cents. (*Uniform with Rolfe's Shakespeare.*)

The carefully arranged editions of "The Merchant of Venice" and other of Shakespeare's plays prepared by Mr. William J. Rolfe for the use of students will be remembered with pleasure by many readers, and they will welcome another volume of a similar character from the same source, in the form of the "Select Poems of Oliver Goldsmith," edited with notes fuller than those of any other known edition, many of them original with the editor.—*Boston Transcript.*

Mr. Rolfe is doing very useful work in the preparation of compact hand-books for study in English literature. His own personal culture and his long experience as a teacher give him good knowledge of what is wanted in this way.—*The Congregationalist*, Boston.

Mr. Rolfe has prefixed to the Poems selections illustrative of Goldsmith's character as a man, and grade as a poet, from sketches by Macaulay, Thackeray, George Colman, Thomas Campbell, John Forster, and Washington Irving. He has also appended at the end of the volume a body of scholarly notes explaining and illustrating the poems, and dealing with the times in which they were written, as well as the incidents and circumstances attending their composition. — *Christian Intelligencer*, N. Y.

The notes are just and discriminating in tone, and supply all that is necessary either for understanding the thought of the several poems, or for a critical study of the language. The use of such books in the school-room cannot but contribute largely towards putting the study of English literature upon a sound basis; and many an adult reader would find in the present volume an excellent opportunity for becoming critically acquainted with one of the greatest of last century's poets.—*Appleton's Journal*, N. Y.

PUBLISHED BY HARPER & BROTHERS, NEW YORK.

☞ *The above works are for sale by all booksellers, or they will be sent by* HARPER & BROTHERS *to any address on receipt of price as quoted. If ordered sent by mail, 10 per cent. should be added to the price to cover cost of postage.*

THOMAS GRAY.

SELECT POEMS OF THOMAS GRAY. Edited, with Notes, by WILLIAM J. ROLFE, A.M., formerly Head Master of the High School, Cambridge, Mass. Illustrated. Square 16mo, Paper, 40 cents; Cloth, 56 cents. (*Uniform with Rolfe's Shakespeare.*)

Mr. Rolfe has done his work in a manner that comes as near to perfection as man can approach. He knows his subject so well that he is competent to instruct all in it; and readers will find an immense amount of knowledge in his elegant volume, all set forth in the most admirable order, and breathing the most liberal and enlightened spirit, he being a warm appreciator of the divinity of genius.—*Boston Traveller.*

The great merit of these books lies in their carefully edited text, and in the fulness of their explanatory notes. Mr. Rolfe is not satisfied with simply expounding, but he explores the entire field of English literature, and therefrom gathers a multitude of illustrations that are interesting in themselves and valuable as a commentary on the text. He not only instructs, but stimulates his readers to fresh exertion; and it is this stimulation that makes his labor so productive in the school-room.—*Saturday Evening Gazette*, Boston.

Mr. William J. Rolfe, to whom English literature is largely indebted for annotated and richly illustrated editions of several of Shakespeare's Plays, has treated the "Select Poems of Thomas Gray" in the same way—just as he had previously dealt with the best of Goldsmith's poems.—*Philadelphia Press.*

Mr. Rolfe's edition of Thomas Gray's select poems is marked by the same discriminating taste as his other classics.—*Springfield Republican.*

Mr. Rolfe's rare abilities as a teacher and his fine scholarly tastes enable him to prepare a classic like this in the best manner for school use. There could be no better exercise for the advanced classes in our schools than the critical study of our best authors, and the volumes that Mr. Rolfe has prepared will hasten the time when the study of mere form will give place to the study of the spirit of our literature.—*Louisville Courier-Journal.*

An elegant and scholarly little volume.—*Christian Intelligencer*, N. Y.

PUBLISHED BY HARPER & BROTHERS, NEW YORK.

☞ *The above works are for sale by all booksellers, or they will be sent by* HARPER & BROTHERS *to any address on receipt of price as quoted. If ordered sent by mail, 10 per cent. should be added to the price to cover cost of postage.*

www.ingramcontent.com/pod-product-compliance
Lightning Source LLC
Chambersburg PA
CBHW020250170426
43202CB00008B/310